JUST IN CASE...
making a home
for elderly people

Dedication

I am dedicating this book to the residents and staff of my Residential Home; my husband who was also my business partner; all the members of the local community who gave us so much support and although not mentioned by name will know to whom I refer. And to my children who also supported me and, together with close friends, persuaded me to write this book

JUST IN CASE...
making a home
for elderly people

Pat Howard

Illustrations by Maggie Guillon

Third Age Press
London 2000

Third Age Press

ISBN 1 898576 22 X ✓
First edition

Third Age Press Ltd, 2000
Third Age Press, 6 Parkside Gardens
London SW19 5EY
Managing Editor Dianne Norton

© Pat Howard

Illustrations © by Maggie Guillon
Cover design by Dianne Norton

Layout design by Dianne Norton
Printed and bound in Great Britain
by Intype

CONTENTS

continued >>>>

INTRODUCTION

JUST IN CASE . . .

They had all turned green! I blinked and looked again. Still green.

I glanced quickly at those sitting either side of me. Nothing wrong there it appeared. They were sipping their sherries, gulping their beers and throwing back the whisky. Most importantly their faces were a normal, old person's colour.

I looked again at those of my residents who were seated opposite to me in the pub. Even more green than before! I was being silly it must be a trick of the light or a figment of my over-active imagination. The words 'salmonella', 'staphylococci' and 'botulism' danced before my eyes. Surely not! It couldn't possibly be! Could it? We were always so careful, adhered so rigidly to all the rules and regulations concerning food preparation and serving. We weren't just careful, but were neurotically so.

I looked back to those arranged either side of me. Still normal so it couldn't possibly be food poisoning. Relief flooded over me. But this time my glance travelled in a greater arc, taking in the wider view and the Great Outside.

We were seated in a pub built beside a canal with a series of locks. The lock was full and in effect, it was high tide and nature was playing one of those little tricks it felt duty bound to play upon us each time we ventured forth from the safety of the Home.

I think the expression is, 'the wind got up'. Got up? It had, within the space of a few minutes, changed from being a warm gentle breeze into a gale force eight wind which, even as we sat there, was whipping up the surface water into frenzied waves. I could see that the eyes of my residents facing the window were on a level with that heaving mass.

They were feeling seasick! Oh good, that's all right then. No it wasn't! Whatever was I thinking about — turn their faces away. Quickly!

I should not have really been surprised. Every working moment of my staffs' and my own day were geared towards making our residents' lives happy, interesting, safe and as pain-free as possible. But a certain law dictated that as soon as we had cracked or solved any untoward situation then, 'blink', and it would change again. Hours of thought and preparation could be swept away in an instant. Therefore plans a b c going on x y and z were always up our sleeves — *just in case* — so that in a crisis one could be pulled out of the bag and put into operation as soon as possible.

This was only possible with the backup of dedicated staff, my husband and support from the entire community — doctors, district nurses and all the other medical teams in the area, social workers and the kindness of the locals and of course the residents' relations.

I first opened my Home in 1990. For the Christmases of years one and two I wrote diaries of events etc of the preceding year, for the interest of my staff. I had intended doing so forever but LIFE got in the way and I never seemed to have time to finish the jottings that I started each summer. So, based on those two and the fragments of further years, here is a compilation of all the different emotions experienced in our Home during that time.

Although around 80% of people live to the end of their lives in their own home, or that of a relative, some cannot, so — *just in case* — it is essential to provide a pleasing environment that can care for and support them with dignity.

Each resident came to us with their own personal entourage, made up of sons, daughters, in-laws, friends, medical teams (doctors, chiropodists, opticians etc) and sometimes spouses fanning out behind them.

In the ensuing pages maybe prospective residents and their families can glean a little insight into what life is like in a communal home. Future carers may get an extra understanding of what caring really means — caring of the whole person.

As with everything else, it is often only the bad examples of which we hear, read or see. Good Homes are pretty thick on the ground and maybe, after reading these pages, for whatever reason, a degree of comfort can be extracted! We really do care.

But I digress! Back to Nature and another coffee/drinks outing.

Lovely weather — an opportunity to go out, so let's find a pub in a scenic position for morning coffee. 'In or out?' I ask my residents through the car windows upon arrival. 'Out', they chorus in unison, their faces uplifted to the warmth of the sun. My carers and I trundle out sufficient numbers of chairs, tables and parasols from inside the pub and then remove the residents from cars, transfer into wheelchairs and onto appropriate chairs.

'Everybody happy?'

'Yes.'

'Any problems?'

'No.' Right. Into the pub, place orders and skip happily back outside again. Wonderful!

'We cannot sit out here,' they cry with one voice. 'We must go inside.'

They could hardly be seen, submerged as they were under a huge black cloud of flies, mosquitoes, gnats — whatever had been up there, were now down here. My helpers and I groaned, slowly we picked up the tables, chairs etc and transferred the residents back into wheelchairs, negotiated tight bends and narrow doorways and so on, back into the pub. Hardly worth bothering now — it was nearly lunchtime.

Funnily enough 'the plague of locusts' never did attack, surprising really — obviously that certain Someone had somehow overlooked that one . . .

PS: All the humans in the book have been given fictitious names

Just in case

JIGSAWS

FINDING THE WHOLE PERSON

'Does anyone know where this comes from?' asked the vicar, holding up a crucifix, about a foot high and made out of old planks and scrap wood. No one answered.

'It came out of Belsen', was his reply.

'Yes,' said a quiet voice from a gentleman sitting to my left. 'I was there just after the war.' Until that moment none of us in the Home were aware that he had been to that dreadful place or what part he played in the aftermath. He had never spoken of it before, and never referred to it again. And so another piece of his personal jigsaw fitted into place.

When a new resident or respite visitor arrived at the Home, their relations and social workers provided us with background information. A doctor from the local practise called to check them over and so, in theory, we were provided with the new arrival's social and medical history and, based on that knowledge we were able to draw up their personal care plans. Usually we had insight into the interests, hobbies, family background and backup and their emotional state. In practice, initially, the plan was only a skeleton and it was during the ensuing weeks and months that the body was built little by little onto that framework.

A lot of the information came from the residents themselves — words tumbling out of some mouths while others were more reticent, remote, waiting until they felt they could fully trust us with knowledge of themselves. Others, more confused, had to rely on their loved ones to build up pictures of their pasts for us. And for our part, we could only look at their beautiful smiles and gentleness and imagine for ourselves the sort of parent or neighbour they had been until perhaps only a short while ago.

So when did we learn most of this extra information? Mostly when the residents were being got-up or put to bed by the carers. Washing, bathing, creaming, tucking-up in bed, the essential one-to-one, the reminiscences, the prides, joys, agonies, bereavements. When laughter and tears and worries are so much easier to share in the privacy of one's bedroom than in the general lounge. This was when untoward changes to their bodies were noticed, reported and, if necessary, acted upon

It is essential that carers have time to give solely to one person. A carer doing nothing physical, just listening or talking, is certainly not wasting time. With or without knowing it gentle counselling is taking place, stacking up information for a future moment when that knowledge may be of infinite use. Anything relevant to a resident's good health, whether it be physical or emotional, was reported to the manager to add to the appropriate section of that person's care plan. In addition good verbal communication also played an important part.

It was therefore equally important that those who were able-bodied had their prime time too and were not overlooked in the business of looking after those who needed more assistance and that there was time to spare for them.

Behind the shrunken bodies and wrinkled skins of my residents were real people. It was easy for us to remember that when working with them continually, their personalities bubbling to the surface but not so easy for a visitor, especially a young visitor, going into the lounge or dining room and catching them mid catnap! It is so easy to dismiss them as being of no importance. Those who could no longer voice opinions, wheelchair bound for whatever reason — those were the ones who tended to be patronised the more. In most cases they knew exactly what was going on around them.

'Wave to me, wave to me', invited a visiting gentleman in a voice reserved for talking to little children, to a lady resident as she was being wheeled away from the dining table. After she had gone I returned to the table wanting to shout 'how dare you patronise that lady', but he hadn't been intentionally unkind and wasn't even aware that he was. Instead I asked him and the others there if they realised she had been a brilliant business woman working in a predominantly mans world? Backbone of the local chapel, chairman, president of various organisations. It was she who (unheralded) looked after any villagers who hit the bad times in days past. She didn't tell us, but her daughter did. In her mid-80s, she had a stroke and had to retire, and she was still a wonderful lady.

What other 'real' people did we have? Well, there was the chairman of the local parish council, football and cricket captains, very many with expertise gained from working all their lives in the motor and engineering industries, businessmen, soldiers, sailors, airmen. They worked down the mines and they worked on the fields. To mention but a few. Most of them were husbands and fathers.

Always more ladies. In fact many more than there were gentlemen. The life expectancy of the male is generally less than the female but we are still in the outer extremities of the catchment area of the two world wars when so many young men were killed leaving a tremendous imbalance of the sexes.

Girls grew up with all that untapped energy which went into raising families. So much to give — every committee in the land, for many years, held up by those indomitable females and soon, sadly, they too will have disappeared.

And what of the ladies in the Home? Mostly wives and mothers but a fair smattering of spinsters too.

The war took its toll on them too. Bombed out, having to share — not enough room, families evacuated to the unknown. One was a bus driver, one a heavy goods vehicle driver, they worked in the factories and on the land, ran post offices. Foreign lady living in a foreign land during the war, and the mother of a young son taken prisoner — however did they cope?

Wives whose husbands were in the forces, often bringing up their families alone, looking after parents and grandparents at the same time. In one case a husband was lost at sea for weeks, presumed dead, but happily not so. How did she cope with that? One a wife of a government adviser, another a nun. There were diplomat's wife, secretaries, dress-makers. The teacher who qualified as a horticulturist but in predominantly a man's world of 60 year's ago, never realised her ambition and always regretted it. The housemaid who worked for a short time at Balmoral and one Christmas danced with King George VI, our Queen's father. Several nurses, one of whom also went into Belsen after the war. No, she didn't tell us either, it was her son who did so after her death. And so on and so on. They all kept homes going in the face of great adversity. All of this information was built up little by little.

A lot of my day was spent in the office, on the 'phone, shopping, collecting prescriptions or visiting prospective residents and respite visitors in their own homes or hospital. But once a day and every day I had my own one-to-one with the residents, preparing and serving them their breakfasts and again this proved a good yardstick for comparisons. They usually kept to their own routine and so any difference to the norm could surreptitiously be looked into ie., why stay in bed when they always got up, difference or slight loss of movement, appetite, brightness of eye etc. Relatively easy for most to say how they felt but what if their speech was too fragmented and their brain too confused? We all needed to constantly subconsciously assess.

If time allowed on a sunny day, I would take some of the residents out for a ride. Sometimes the route would take us to a village or past a house where one of them used to live. We tried to arrange it so that friends sat next to each other. The two ladies who played at being 'stags at bay' with their walking frames on hairdressing mornings loved it. They had become very great friends — both matriarchal ladies, similar backgrounds, they didn't need to speak much, just be close. Both were fairly deaf, so conversations were difficult anyway. No, they just sat side by side, holding hands and enjoying being taken out together.

Being somewhat confused did not stop one gentleman being an excellent guide. He sat beside me in the front passenger seat and plied me with information about the local vicinity from his childhood to the present day. It was so enlightening and entertaining that it wasn't until afterwards I wondered how accurate it was — or whether he had made it up as we went along! It didn't matter as we both enjoyed the ride.

One of the favourite rides, just the right distance away, was to a ridge of hills. As we drove through the lovely village at the bottom and then slowly wound our way upwards, everyone except one 'oohed' and 'aahed' at the beautiful scenery. The one exception was too busy marvelling at the cats' eyes and the texture of the roads surface! Her eyes were riveted to the centre of the road, the natural beauty of the area totally ignored. During the war and afterwards she had driven buses along the rural roads of Hampshire. Although a different county this particular piece of countryside rang bells in her memory. Her one topic of conversation was how she wished cats eyes had been invented and installed in those far off days. She mentioned it at least two or three times going up the hill, and two or three times going down again.

Another lady reminisced how as a young girl she had stayed there with an aunt and spent a lot of her time rolling down the slopes.

'Look at the sheep, the lambs, the kites', I would cry.

'Oh yes', they would reply, giving them a cursory glance. I don't know why I bothered with conversation, immersed as they were in their own thoughts and happy memories.

'Once a year in the summer', said another lady, 'we held a church service up there. It was lovely.'

'This was a wonderful place for courting', said another. I got the impression her memories were even more delightful than the previous lady's.

'It was good in the snow. We slipped, slid and tobogganed down here', exclaimed another. And then added rather needlessly, 'It was a long time ago.'

Trees fully dressed in their summer or autumn clothes was the subject which delighted another gentleman. A copse or avenue of trees was even better. Wilf was almost blind, but he could see great splurges of colour and loved the open air. We came to rest at the peak of the hill, overlooking the valley. We opened the doors. Everyone took a deep breath, said what lovely air it was and should we have an ice cream. But Wilf always asked the same question when we were parked in that spot. 'I wonder how many strata of rock are beneath us?' he mused. No one was able to answer that question or even make an intelligent conversation around it. It didn't matter. He wasn't into replies — he was into memories.

All his working life he had been a miner. He knew which stratum was which. The victim of an underground accident, he had almost lost a foot. The physical problems more or less healed over the years but the mental scars never fully faded. Up until the time of his death, in his nineties, he still from time to time suffered nightmares. Always the same one.

As we sat on top of the hills he would start to talk about his determination that his two sons should not go down the mines. He was so proud of them that tears would trickle down his cheeks as once again he would outline their successful careers. Wilf hadn't failed them. The widow of one lived nearby constantly visiting, loving, supporting, teasing and supplying him with his beloved tapes. On our outings not only could he see the trees he also remembered how good it was to be above ground.

On the way back in the appropriate season we would indulge in one of my favourite past times — as long as a certain lady was sitting beside me. It was called 'find the field of beans'. The exotic perfume would waft into the car — but from where? Not necessarily from fields adjacent to the roads. Both my resident and I came from farming backgrounds and to us there was no finer perfume than that of field beans. The trouble was one had to be in the right position, down wind, to catch a whiff of it. Other residents must have wondered what we were looking for as we hurtled around the country lanes, noses jutting out of windows as we tried to pin down that elusive fragrance.

The route that I have described was always very popular. On this type of outing it was possible to be spontaneous so if anyone wanted to go anywhere specifically (within reason) it could be arranged. Usually they didn't — they were just pleased to be seeing the sights.

One should never presume anything when running a Home for elderly people. Many a time when I thought a certain idea was good because it would be of specific interest to a certain person it turned out to be not the least bit interesting!

Ben arrived at the Home having led a very sheltered, insular life. The priority during his youth had been to assist his father with running the farm so he'd missed a lot of schooling which was common in the 1920's. His reading abilities were well below par and we understood from the family that he had been treated rather like the village idiot in those far away days. But the longer we knew him we realised that in fact he was quite well informed. An idiot he most certainly wasn't gleaning a lot of his information from the television and enjoying listening to and partaking in interesting and intelligent conversations!

But in the first week of his arrival that particular piece of the jigsaw had not been put into place. He was in desperate need of new spectacles so I made an appointment with the local optician and from her found that he could at least read the alphabet easily! Afterwards, having 10 minutes to spare before lunch I took him the scenic route home. Over the canals and along by the hedgerows which had very recently been 'laid' — he would surely be interested. Probably used to do some himself. As we drew level to these clever works of art Ben turned his back on them and said, 'I understand the housing market is in a precipitous state at the moment' (as indeed it was at that time)! Whoops, I think he was trying to tell me something like 'Don't assume anything until you know me better and don't believe what you have heard about me. Judge for yourself'!

Jigsaws? Some pictures were easy to assemble. Light, dark — contrasts — easy to see where each piece fitted. While others — no definite outline, just a blur, shaded and so difficult to piece together. With some residents (and I suspect all to some extent) we never did get the complete picture.

ROUTINES

HAIRY BUT NECESSARY

'I've never seen anything like it', gasped a carer, clinging to the side of the cupboard and shaking visibly. Monday morning shifts were not her norm — she was filling in for someone else — and I got the distinct feeling that she would not be repeating that nicety.

Monday mornings had to be got through, in order that the rest of the week could be happy and contented. Why? Because . . . Monday mornings were hairdressing mornings.

No hurry? No urgency? No way!

This was vanity, being top of the pile, first in the queue stuff, all rolled into one! Everyone wanted to be first and one thought very carefully before selecting the one who was to be last – or even second! Why on earth did it matter — no one was going anywhere? But it did matter. This was the battling female at her best.

Before the hairdressing area was built upstairs, it would all take place in the bathroom downstairs. In those days (when the average age of our residents was younger), they would wake early and request breakfast early, in order to be first in the queue. The idea was actually to fetch them from their rooms in an orderly fashion, when it was their turn to have their hair shampooed, set, blow-dried, permed or cut. It seldom worked out that way, — legs broke forth into a shuffle, wheelchairs were self-propelled and seats rammed into cavities half the desired size. Two ladies in particular, at other times the dearest of friends, vied for the front line. They were like stags at bay, with the legs of their Zimmer frames entwined like horns locked in mortal combat as they mixed their metaphors and jostled for pole position.

Actually, I joke. It was good to see. Thank goodness these women still had enough self-respect to want to look smart and attractive and thank goodness they still had the energy and willpower to virtually kill to be so. Thank goodness their fighting spirit hadn't been quashed.

All that changed (not the vanity aspect — that never diminished) with the advent of the hairdressing area. Mainly because it was upstairs and most had to be escorted in the lift to get there. This didn't stop those whose bedrooms were on that floor being competitive, but after '93/'94 ish, the ladies coming into the Home, due to Care in the Community, were more elderly and had less fight. But they still wanted their hair done. Correction, they didn't actually want it done, but they needed the end result and would still be prepared to go through hell and high water to achieve the desired effect.

They all slept through Monday afternoon, so exhausted were they from the morning's fun and games. Our hairdresser was most forbearing and must have gone home with her head reeling. As did that particular carer after her one-off session.

Tuesdays were marginally more laid back. Alternate Tuesday mornings was Holy Communion, which commands a chapter all to itself. Every Holy Communion service was a variation on the theme of that particular service.

Tuesday afternoons were another time to titillate the vanities and wellbeing of the ladies and, this time, gentlemen also. Because Tuesday afternoon was hand massage and nail manicure time. For a small fee, the British Red Cross representative performed this happiest of tasks getting through a third to a half of the residents each week. She kept her own lists and no one jumped her queue! This really was a personal service and of great value to the receiver. It was also an important task. Jagged, uneven nails can rip through wafer-thin skin in no time at all, leaving a wound wide open to infection. In between times, it was important that the carers kept nails even and short and in good order. Long, unattended nails, going into places they shouldn't go, also harboured germs and quickly spread disease and infection.

There was more to it — the massage soothed away inner tensions, leaving the mind open to receive and enjoy this most pleasant of conversationalists. The lady from the Red Cross was widely travelled, had many and varied interests, lived locally and knew intimately many of the residents, their relations and friends. This was one-to-one time when each resident in turn was the centre of attention and the conversation was intimate and then, when the subject matter allowed, those on either side could be drawn into the conversation. Yes, Tuesday afternoon was a very good afternoon.

Wednesday afternoons once a month were also good afternoons. On that afternoon our residents attended a club in the village for the over sixties (to come into its own later). This left three of four Wednesday afternoons in the month for visiting entertainers, should the occasion arise. And also, men's barber time. No, the men's coiffures were not forgotten either. Initially looked after by the same lady hairdresser who attended to the ladies, until a phenomenon occurred. We had four full-time male residents and sometimes five if the respite visitor were of that sex too. Something needed to be done! So, every month to six weeks the hairdressing area became a barber's shop. Whether all the men needed their hair cutting or not they all went and talked to the barber without any hindrance at all from those women!

And so to Thursday. Thursday was different. Thursday was do it yourself day. Each afternoon the residents gyrated and exercised their limbs to the music of their former days. Fully trained in the benefits of this kind of movement, the young lady who led the class encouraged, enticed and wheedled the residents into getting their legs and arms into appropriate positions. Gently raising or lowering limbs, catching and throwing balls, singing along to tapes of earlier years – it all sounded very therapeutic. When my grandson stayed he acted as ball boy. I don't know how they coped when he wasn't there as he never seemed to stop running after dropped balls. Exercises took place both inside — and out, when the weather allowed. No one escaped by sitting on the patio under the umbrellas and pretending to be asleep!

More seriously, on alternate Thursday mornings, the physiotherapist came in privately to exercise and walk those with stroke-related problems and/or disabilities. Checking out new problems, advising, demonstrating to staff the correct hold or manoeuvre or massage for each individual problem — another layer of support and another safety net for the residents.

Of course not everyone attended all these functions and outings. Some stayed away through a current illness or general ill health. Others felt they needed a rest or were not interested in that specific event, preferring to stay in their rooms, reading quietly, writing or watching television. It was their choice.

The routine of the week was important to the residents. They knew where they were — what day it was (well, sometimes). Stability.

The importance of the oiling and exercising as many parts of the body, mind and spirits as possible can not be underlined too much. Creaking joints, feelings and voices, all needed to do their 'knees bend, arms stretch' routine so that the new hairstyle and manicured nails and immaculately laundered dresses could sit more joyously on and around their bodies.

For vanity did not seem to wither with age. The ladies liked to look smart at all times — wear co-ordinating colour schemes, hair neatly arranged, faces made-up, perfumed. As did the men (like to look smart). If a relative arrived out of the blue, they were clean and smart enough already to be wafted off for a lunch or a home visit. It was what they all expected. Some preferred smart, casual clothes, but mostly it depended upon their dress sense and what they were used to wearing before they came into the Home full-time. Sometimes clothing had to be adapted for ease and quickness of use. Zipped up trousers were replaced by 'joggers' with elasticated waists, hold-ups or stockings instead of tights, whatever was easier to get up or down quickly! Trousers and skirts with elasticated waists being more comfortable for expanding waistlines. Skirts and tops being easier to get on and off, rather than complete dresses, and so on, with those whose movements were restricted. But whatever they wore, the outfit still had to be smart and acceptable to the wearer.

Both sexes liked to check themselves out in the mirror in their rooms before joining the group downstairs. On one side of the lift was a very large mirror in front of which went a lot of surreptitious preening. None more so than from Geoffrey who came to live with us, sadly, for only a few months. He came to us with a very small, depleted wardrobe, which my staff soon built up by bringing in various garments in good condition which their husbands no longer needed. (Whether the husbands knew they no longer needed them, I'm not sure!) His self-esteem mounted by the day. Never had he looked so good. Washed, shaven, good haircut, he thrived in his new outfits and the general ambience of the Home. Overwhelmed by his new good looks, he could not resist gazing with admiration into the lift mirror, straightening his tie and smoothing back his hair.

'I'm the smartest man here, aren't I?' Geoffrey would gently ask or state to his escort without the slightest nuance of boastfulness in his voice. Not many men could get away with that sort of talk in a predominantly female establishment! My goodness he lived dangerously! But coming from him it was good to hear. For the first time in his life (we knew his background) he was smart, esteemed and revelled in the knowledge. No one could take those moments of glory and self-satisfaction away. Indeed, no one ever wanted to — he was the most gentle and kindest of gentlemen. A great favourite with the other men — and went down very well with the ladies too! As he left the lounge each evening to go to his room he would raise his arm, lightly salute and bow to each of them in turn, calling them all by name. He was lovely and so innocent.

'Hello Dad. Fancy seeing you here.' Fancy indeed! Sometimes Edward saw his elder brother, instead of his father, which was equally worrying, our resident being 91 himself, that is. Edward had very poor eyesight and presumably just made out the outline of his own reflection, which must have resembled that of his father, as he remembered him. Most times, while travelling up or down in the lift, he indulged in this conversation with the mirror.

'Haven't seen you lately' or 'How are you today?' but mostly it was expressions of astonishment and amazement that he uttered. Much cheaper than attending a séance and these encounters had no adverse effect upon him whatsoever. We did wonder at first. But no! He enjoyed the moment and then struck it out of his mind until the next time, when he would take fresh delight in the impromptu meeting. It would seem that mirrors have more than one function in life!

'Should I walk like this, dear?' she asked, bent double and leaning heavily and precariously on her stick.

'No, please walk naturally. There is no need to act — just be yourself. The doctor will see how much assistance you need.'

It was assessment day for Sybil, whose family had applied for extra funding, and a 'neutral' doctor was due to arrive later in the day.

'Oh, all right' she snorted. She liked a good play-act.

Half an hour later — 'Should I walk like this, dear?'

'No!'

Many, many half hours later, complete with an equal number of repeat performances, the same conversation was taking place right up until the time of the appointment. There really was no need for exaggeration or pretence, she needed a lot of support, day and night. Apart from in one area. The minute she laid back, whether it be on the bed, or in the bath, she would swing her legs upwards in one continuous sweep, until they were almost touching the back of her head (she didn't learn that at keep fit on Thursday afternoons). It was quite remarkable because she could normally only shuffle along. As Sybil was the only person in the Home (and that probably included most of the staff, as well as the residents) who could perform this feat, she liked to show it off as often as possible. A bit of one-upmanship!

I should have remembered her party piece. The doctor made his entrance, and she immediately went into acting mode. Body quivering. Voice quavering. The doctor and I held a silent conversation above her head. He had seen it all before. Then, 'Can you get on the bed, dear?' he kindly enquired. I helped her slowly into a recumbent position.

So proud of what she could do with her legs. 'Look at me', she shrieked. The doctor's face was a picture. There she was, flat on her back, peddling her legs round and round, chortling with laughter.

What a pity her memory was so bad and she had forgotten the reason for his visit. He made a hasty retreat, having seen all that he needed and more, I suspected, than was required.

Mirror, mirror on the wall . . . whether it be in the bedroom, lift or bathroom. Not only were our residents proud — and quite rightly so — of their looks and fashions, but some were still very proud of their bodies too. The mirrors in the bathrooms providing the backdrop for them to model, completely naked, in front of them and to admire and delight in how well they were 'preserved', as they called it. This way and that, they slowly swayed. The fact that the mirror was usually steamed over and they had taken their glasses off did not dilute their enthusiasm. I suspect that what they saw were actually memories of an earlier age. What did it matter? If a lady or gentleman, 80, 90 or 99 was still taking that much interest in their body, then you knew that they personally had no intention of popping off quite yet.

Our lady of the swinging legs had no such interest in the mirrors in the bathroom. Sybil had other immediate aims, as soon as she got there — to get into the bath as quickly as possible, lie back, then throw those legs up into the air, one after the other. Up and down, scissors-like.

My carers learnt at a very early stage that one never lent too far over her to help her wash when she was taking a bath! Not if they didn't want to get a big toe stuck up their nose!

FEELINGS . . .

OF FEAR, LOSS & HAPPINESS

(Bereavement – to be robbed of anything valued) [1]

All of our residents came to us in a state of 'bereavement'. No, not necessarily from the recent death of their spouses. Some had had partners who had died many years before. Some had never been married or their fiancés had been killed all those years ago during the two wars.

But what about all those other items of value which one collected as one went through life? What about homes, furniture, neighbours, gardens, pets, familiar sounds and smells, familiar outlooks, streets and voices and in many cases freedom of choice? All those things are of value to all of us at some time in our lives. Maybe never more valued than when sight, hearing and mobility have deteriorated to such an extent that there is great need for everything to be in its place and to know where one is. When you go into full time care directly from your own home, you can be robbed of all of those things in one move.

(1) Chambers 20th Century Dictionary

The reasons for our residents seeking residential care were almost as many as were the number of ladies and gentlemen who lived with us over the years. Admittedly most came because they could no longer fend for themselves, not even with the backup of family, friends, doctors and social services. Not all admitted to being in this state and greatly resented the implications that they were no longer capable of being in control of their lives. Not only were the potential residents unhappy but their families had been reduced to feelings of guilt. In this category most were truly not aware of the problems their families faced. Some were too confused with beginnings of dementia and no longer able to make decisions. Others knew what they should do but did not want to admit defeat.

The restrictions of arthritis, strokes, impaired sight and hearing mostly came to these ladies and gentlemen in later life. They found it difficult to come to terms with these disabilities which brought restrictions to their everyday lives. In some cases they were angry, resentful and frightened and could not cope emotionally. Others were more fatalistic. All were frustrated at the slowing-down process of old age.

Often the physical disabilities made it impracticable and impossible for them to live at home — their own home not lending itself to the requirements of stair lifts, ramps or the space needed for the manoeuvrability of wheelchairs, walking frames and other aids. Steps provided another problem — up to and down from the house or within the home itself. Often nothing wrong with the mind. They could still have lived in their own homes or sheltered accommodation if their hearts had been stronger or if certain limbs did not hang heavily and uselessly by their sides. Or if they could pick up their feet and not trip and fall over most things.

How extra difficult and sad it was for the younger residents no longer able to live in their homes where the wife or husband still resided. How extra difficult it was for the wife or husband whose spouse had been taken into care because they themselves were not physically strong enough, not even with back up, to look after them. Both in a state of semi-bereavement. Life would be so much easier if it were simply 'black or white'. For most of us that grey area in between the two seems to dominate our lives. This applies especially when a husband and wife want/need to go into the same Home and continue to live together. In a perfect 'black or white' world that would be very easy, but what if one partner is more ill or dependent than the other — one needs residential care and the other nursing care? In some cases one spouse may have advance dementia and needs to go to a Home which specifically deals with that illness — and many more variations on that theme. So once more the couple would be parted and sadness enter their lives.

There are many Homes which have dual registration — the County Council register residential homes and the Health Authority register nursing homes — (this was so during the time when I managed my Home), so thus a possibility to look into.

I had very little demand for a husband and wife double room, as mostly one partner had cared for the other, either in their own home or sheltered accommodation, until their death. Other Home owners may not agree with my experience and Homes in cities or towns where there is a large conurbation of population may find they are inundated with requests for double rooms.

Fear featured quite high on the list of reasons for leaving ones own home. Bearing in mind that it is a frightening step to take anyway, going into a strange and alien environment at a most vulnerable time in ones life, one knew that anyone who admitted to being too frightened to continue to live in their own home and opting for communal living had to be very frightened indeed. Frightened to live alone, frightened they would fall, be taken ill in the night, frightened of burglars.

We subsequently discovered that Amelia, who came to us exhausted, sat up all and every night convinced that some-one was trying to get into her house. Although already very old and hampered with arthritis she was still capable of running her own life more or less. Her family was solidly supportive and loving. Initially they were not aware of the sleepless nights and their implications. Then it well and truly manifested itself and they acted immediately. Already a respite visitor to the Home — we had room for her. It was good to see her gain strength, mentally and physically. Secure and safe, sleep came at night to Amelia once again.

Not everyone dreaded going into residential care — far from it! There have been several residents in the Home who arrived because they actually wanted to. Living in a granny flat or with their family or still in their own home alone they had made a self analysis of the situation and decided it was time to move on. As one recounted, 'I thought it was time for me to go into a Home. I needed more help than my family could give me and they had their lives to lead. Although I was very happy with them I reached the stage when I realised I needed 24-hours care and they needed more freedom.' The family sat down together, talked the subject through and made their decision. As their mother she was still an integral part of the family, still loved and respected. She in turn had given them a great gift — the gift of not having to feel guilty! It was her decision. She settled well and became a much loved mother figure to us all.

Although there were general guidelines for admittance, these could only be used as a base, the staff building on them and moulding the Home around the newcomer, letting him or her choose how he or she wanted to make her 'entrance'.

Mostly they chose to have a tea or coffee in their bedroom with the relative who had brought them in, getting their bearings quietly. Maybe they would choose to eat their first meal with the rest of the Home or prefer to eat quietly in their own room. Other times the relative might escort their parent into the lounge for the initial hot drink, drawing those on either side of them into a general conversation with the newcomer and thereby breaking the ice. It took days or even weeks for a newcomer to settle into the routine no matter how loosely that routine was adhered to — again, it being just a base. So many new faces to get to know and so many names to try and remember. The first day is the most exhausting. Torn apart with mixed emotions, stretching them to the limit. During early evening a warm, relaxing bath followed by their favourite drink and then an early bed, is what is most requested. As soon as the new resident is comfortable and asleep a phone call to their loved ones is always a good idea. Just to let them know that so far, all is well, so — switch off, relax and have a good night's sleep too. With many carers that will be the first good night's rest without fear of disturbance that they will have had for months, going on years.

For the staff, it was an important time of building bridges for the newcomer . From old to new, giving strength and understanding, taking interest, exchanging confidences, joking, teasing and caring. Finding out what routine was best for that individual and making them smile and laugh and feel safe again.

We all wear masks to varying degrees, covering fright, embarrassment etc and never more so than when one leaves the old familiar routine and enters a Home. It made no difference whether it was for respite or full time residency. The walking through the front door for the first time is frightening. What if no one speaks to me or understands me? What if I cannot hear them or see adequately where I am going? What if I don't like the food, if the bed is uncomfortable, if I cannot have a milky drink at night — the one which I am used to? Once in a while residents have arrived wearing no masks at all. Their faces deeply etched in fright and fear. Others have come in determined to make their mark — not to be pushed around as they wrongly anticipate they might. Whereas others just wanted to blend in — anything for a quiet life.

Happiness for the Home was seeing the real person emerge from behind whatever façade the new respite visitor or new resident adopted to help survive the agonising fear of the unknown — mostly hampered by ailing sight, hearing, memory and immobility. The façades varied from being almost totally introverted and shy to being very assertive and extroverted. One gentle lady came in from time to time for respite care. Each time she worked off her anxieties by expending an awful lot of physical energy before she felt she could settle down again and get on with living. To get from her bedroom she would, metaphorically, trampoline out of bed, slide down the banisters, backward somersault through the reception area, cartwheel along the passage, skip through the lounge, trip down the ramp into the garden, collapse into a sun chair, pick up the nearest bumble bee and proceed to stroke it. Well, yes, that was a slight exaggeration (apart from the bumble bee, which really did happen) — but that was how it felt to the assistant who had lurched alongside her, arms outstretched to catch her, herself exhausted trying to keep up.

Unhappiness was saying goodbye to respite visitors, not knowing if or when we would see them again.

It was always a source of amazement to all of us how well, on the whole, the residents lived amicably together. They came from various backgrounds — social, financial, educational and religious, the main bond being that most came from the village or nearby villages or town and so had a lot of local knowledge and background — or their relatives did.

They were also subconsciously sharing feelings of bereavement and could therefore identify and understand each others attitudes, could understand the cavity carved out within each other that no one nor nothing could fill when a spouse (and often best friend) dies after a marriage of anything up to 50 or 60 years. Even attitudes which were not always acceptable could be understood and overlooked. Bereavement was a great common communicator.

It is so easy for the younger person to say they understand bereavement. They understand their own level of bereavement, even if widowed young, and all the pressures which they have to endure and overcome. When in the later stages of ones life and bereaved one cannot, at the drop of a hat, go out for coffee, have a hair-do or meet friends for lunch to cheer oneself up and be strengthened — neither party, the bereaved nor the comforter, in most cases being able to drive or walk far. Friends — those who are left and mostly very elderly too — cannot likewise drop everything and visit. No reason for getting up in the mornings and not much reason for cooking proper meals. No children to have to get to school. Sometimes even their children have died.

Not only did the trauma of vacating a beloved home feature highly in a potential (or new) resident's list of unhappinesses, but also the disposal of its contents. Furniture, pictures, ornamentals — who should have them, what should we do with them, were the immediate family's thoughts and problems? Small pieces of furniture and memorabilia could be accommodated in the resident's room, making it more personal and 'loveable'. But what about the large pieces of furniture — the suites and individual pieces? Furniture, cutlery, china and crockery which had been part of their lives for years, going back to when their children were young and when their spouses were still alive. All the memories that they evoked.

Often residents had to be whisked into a home or hospital for their own physical good with no time to discuss or resolve whom should have what or where it should go. So much for the carers to do, to read through, to sort out, and so many impossible decisions to be made. Even if there was endless time to communicate about the emotive subject, it did not necessarily bring about happy solutions. One person's treasures were another's rubbish. Family heirlooms and antiques can usually be accommodated within the family but what about the rest of the furniture? The beauty and value as beheld by the resident is often out-dated, rickety or are pieces which no one wants to give house room. Not only that but the children's homes are usually already full to overflowing. Sometimes grandchildren are pleased to receive bits until they can afford more modern, fashionable ones, only to throw out the grandparent's furniture as soon as possible (at their peril!).

As with everything else, the sooner the lines of communication on this subject are forged the better. But even that doesn't always work. Some residents wanted to know exactly who had what and where the residue went and others closed their minds and ears to it, trying to wipe the memory away. Then weeks later would wish they had done exactly the opposite — by which time it was too late. Sitting in their rooms now with plenty of time, it was so easy to think and re-think who should have what and why didn't they. Or even worse — where are they now because I want them all back! One of the most difficult times physically, mentally and emotionally for the family and certainly an emotional time for the resident.

Of course it wasn't always peace and love to mankind in the Home. Jumping to wrong conclusions was quite a common pastime — often due to inadequate hearing and then gleefully adding their own interpretations of a situation for maximum effect. These annoyances could simmer on for days, growing in momentum. Difficult to sort out when no one seemed to know the original cause or who had said what and why — another reason for staff knowing the residents well. Some of the upsets were caused by medical problems. A chest infection or cold could topple a person off their well-balanced programme of drugs and of course there were many, many other reasons. Hallucinations on rare occasions set in — the residents seeing someone who wasn't actually present, hearing voices. That, as you could imagine, could often start arguments.

Jealousies sometimes surfaced. More visitors, new clothes, more agile, more outings — anything could trigger it off. Usually those feelings did not seem to last too long, thanks mainly to the staff, assessing the situation and acting in a positive way to make the aggrieved more content and accepting of the situation.

There were pockets of annoyance and discontent. Sometimes even visitors annoyed other residents inadvertently or the television may have been on too loud or not loud enough. Sometimes they were real and big problems and other times they were trivial, made-up and of no consequence or substance. Someone just felt like annoying someone else. In the real world they experienced all those emotions so why not (although hopefully to a lesser extent) in a Home? At least they and we knew they were still alive! Some loved it and secretly engineered trouble (not wishing to appear to stir). To others it was cruel and unkind and if this happened, it had to be quickly nipped in the bud. The clever part for the staff was knowing at what stage a situation changed from stimulation and acceptable behaviour, to a situation that would cause great unhappiness and following on from that, physical and emotional problems.

There was never a dull moment and it seemed as if there was never enough time to truly relax! We were so grateful that we usually had a handful of quiet, unassuming ladies in residence who would not intentionally cause anyone any unhappiness. *Blessed are the peacemakers!* Every Home needs them. They were the ones who smoothed over irritations caused by others. They were the ones who placated and tactfully changed subject matters when things got 'hairy'. They were the ones who had a greater interest in the running of the Home and were interested in the staff — their happiness or their worries. And apropos nothing in particular, they always seemed to be the ones who were great knitters. Many of the gentlemen were likewise calming influences — often seeing a problem from a different angle. They too were great tacticians. They were also great teasers and well experienced in the art of 'sending-up' and 'stirring'! Mostly the ladies enjoyed this — we needed the men to balance things out. The ones who didn't, I suspected, were ones who didn't have brothers! But wherever they sat, male or female, one could guarantee that the area around the peacemakers was more tranquil than the rest of the room.

Although the lounge was the hub of the house to the residents, they did not have to be there all of their waking time. Some did because it was preferable to them. Then there were those who spent nearly all their time in their rooms — and many who used both. With one or two exceptions all the residents benefited from some level of communal life.

It had to be accepted though that someone who had lived on their own for years with very few visitors could not cope with long conversations. They were out of practise and could not sustain the energy required to talk for very long. If they felt like that it would be cruel to enforce it. Noise too, if you are unused to it, can be tiring as can general chatter and clatter.

One had to be very aware of wanderings and worries that occurred in the night. The new residents needing extra overseeing. Waking up, being disorientated — where were they? Furniture not in the same familiar position (always extra difficult for the partially sighted), window not on the same wall, nor the door, nor the bed. Very upsetting until they got their bearings. As long as they remembered to ring if needing anything, not so bad but so often initially they would forget (or not like to) to use the bell so would have to lie and worry until the member of staff paid her routine visit.

One hears the uninitiated berating the dirty habits of elderly people. In almost all cases these are not intentional or desired. Elderly feeble muscles, lack of control, medication and memories play a large part. Always difficult for them in the first days of communal living. So much more attention needed to give confidence and calm the nerves. They certainly would not have dreamt of behaving in such a manner until only a short while before and would be desperately upset if they realised they did now.

From time to time a letter would arrive with the name of the Home, Greenways, being wrongly spelled on the envelope. We have been addressed as 'Strangeways' — no comment. We have been addressed as 'Greenhills'. Nicer, but that always induced those *far away* feelings. And then there was 'Greenwarp'. 'Greenwarp'? Wherever did that come from? No one with half an eye to marketing or advertising would call a care home 'Greenwarp'. It conjured up images of the building slowly sinking under a wave of yellowy-green slime. Yes — well I suppose on a particularly bad day that wasn't too inaccurate a description - or at least that was what it felt like!

One by one our residents would die and leave a gap in our lives. Yes, their rooms were soon filled with new people — residents who would themselves become an integral part of our Home. However, inevitably staff became attached to individuals. After all it was a two-way flow of feelings. Some staff suited some residents better than others but with 30 staff there were always plenty to go around so that no resident need feel that there was no one with whom they could empathise.

When a resident died, more often than not the staff would lose a good friend and confidante. My busiest and most difficult day was that day. Often, having been up since the early hours of the morning dealing with the doctor, undertaker, relations (often already being there) and helping the staff on duty (more often than not, the night staff) wash and change the deceased. Then tidying the bedroom, taking out all the extras which home nursing requires so that when the relation visited the room it was an oasis of peace and tranquility and breaking the news to the other residents one by one in the privacy of their own rooms so they could grieve in private if wished.

Then there was the marathon of ringing my staff who weren't on duty. Giving them the news that was usually expected but still wanting them to know when the resident died so that they did not walk in 'cold' and could grieve privately at home. They were the ones who had looked after the deceased for months or even years and it would have been insulting not to tell them and thank them for making that person's life happy and comfortable in their last years.

'We won't cry', we said. 'It was what they and the family would have wanted. It was right.'

No need for tears. If only!

They were always long, sad days. Each resident would leave behind a specific thought, saying, colour, whatever, in our memories. One gentleman left the fruit bowl he made at day classes for the blind and another visually impaired man carved animals, one of which sat on the mantelpiece. We could never see an arrangement of flowers or dresses in mauve and pink without seeing a certain pretty lady with a smile to match. Staff who had been with me for years shared these feelings. We would no longer hear about late husbands or wives. Never more hear about the Jimmys and Ernests and many more. Matching earrings and necklaces, jigsaw puzzles, knitted dolls with bumble bees on their hats, bible and prayer books on windowsills, Sue Boettcher cats. Cats on calendars, on mats and tea clothes — any cats, anywhere. 'Och!', 'Can I have a ba-na-na?', 'Thanks a million', 'Dry rot and woodworm', 'Have you seen my teeth?', a lady who giggled so much she was always collapsing all over the place — all these conglomerations and many, many more. Maybe none more so than a certain gentleman's smile which, long after he died, like that of Alice's Cheshire cat, lasted on and on and on . . .

ODDITIES
& IMPONDERABLES

Life in the Home had to be one of routine, with certain jobs done at certain times of the day. That way the residents and we the staff knew where we were — well, sometimes!

Dressing, undressing, bathing, washing, creaming, toileting, etc. Interspersed with these were the oddities, all essential to the peaceful ambience of the residents' day. For instance, re-setting the television back to the required programme after bent and arthritic fingers have played havoc with the remote control (a frequent one). Bringing down the sound to an acceptable level featured pretty regularly too. Also picking up dropped books, stitches, teeth and jigsaw pieces. Locating walking sticks from weird and wonderful places. Sometimes we couldn't imagine how they got where they did!

One of the more time-consuming and irritating 'extras' was looking for lost clothes. All clothes were labelled but occasionally by mistake they would end up in the wrong room. This was fairly easily and quickly rectified. Quite rightly the residents got annoyed if an article of clothing was taken away for washing and wasn't returned very quickly. Sometimes the ink wore thin and labels fell off. It was an ongoing job. For the residents, being in control of their clothes and deciding what to wear each day, was an important vital link with their previous life when they were in charge of just about every aspect of it. No wonder they took so much interest and pride in what was left of their past. This applied to the gentlemen as well as the ladies. Stockings, tights, hold-ups, socks — all difficult to label but, fortunately, most females had individual types and colours so these could be sorted and the men had different patterns on their socks.

But sometimes on an off day hours could be wasted looking for articles of clothing that did not actually exist. In desperation I would telephone the daughter and ask whether she had taken this or that piece of clothing home with her and she would often say that she had as that particular item no longer fitted her parent or needed mending! Usually the resident did know about this but had forgotten!

One of our ladies was very clothes conscious and was adamant that a certain dress should have been in her wardrobe. She described it in great detail but no one could remember ever having seen it. But who were we to argue when it came to ladies and their clothes? In desperation I telephoned her daughter having spent too much time already searching for it.

'Oh no', laughed the daughter, 'Mother tried that dress on in the shop last week but it was slightly too big so she didn't buy it but she DID like it.'!!

On another occasion we looked and looked for a stripy skirt. There wasn't one in this lady's wardrobe — nor anyone else's. It was nowhere. In fact, again, no one could remember ever seeing it before. The lady was getting very uptight about it and was wheeled back to her wardrobe for one last look. This she did very reluctantly as she was in a deep sulk by then. The doors were opened and, yes, there it was. Wonderful! Everyone happy and laughing!

No, it wasn't a stripy skirt after all — she didn't actually own one. It was, of course, the skirt with the polka dots all over it — silly us! This lady was totally lucid and usually on the ball so what hope did we have with the slightly confused?

It wasn't just clothes that occasionally went walkabout. Teeth it seemed could travel quite long distances on their own. I have travelled back to churches, often miles away, to crawl and grovel around in the 'third pew from the back on the right' or the 'last seat on the left next to the radiator.' Often I would find them, uppers or lowers, usually wrapped in a napkin or handkerchief but seldom where the owner had said they would be. I have telephoned relatives asking them to look behind flowerpots or down the side of chairs or under the passenger seat of their car to see if the missing teeth could be located. One daughter once rang to say, 'stop looking. They're in my fridge!' We didn't express surprise. The fridge was one of the more acceptable places from which false teeth had been retrieved.

Mostly it was obvious if a denture-wearing person had taken them out — but not always. One of our ladies slotted into the second category and we had more trouble with her than most. Her mouth looked the same with or without teeth. She took them out a lot mostly from habit we assumed as they did not appear to hurt her. It was nothing to find them in her breakfast or teacup. That was relatively all right. No one else could see them. It was at lunchtime that the problem arose when she had a glass as opposed to a china cup. There was nothing more revolting for her fellow diners than seeing a denture floating in a glass of water with all the food particles bubbling up to the surface. There was always something for the carers to sort out. This lady's teeth had a life of their own — they were free spirits!

It was yet another outing. Most of our residents wanted to go as it was a favourite venue and one they had frequented for several years. An excellent programme, entertainment and teas. The tea took place halfway through the programme. There were probably 9 or 10 tables in the hall, each seating approximately 10 people, all of whom were pensioners.

There were an awful lot of dentures present. That dreaded sentence accosted my ears: 'I haven't got my teeth in, dear.' We searched her napkin, discarded crusts off sandwiches, her teacup and her handkerchief but to no avail. I suggested that she probably hadn't been wearing them in the first place but she was adamant that she had. One of my carers said she would go to the kitchen and see if any of the plates that had already been cleared away held the mystery.

'Come back after the show', the organiser said. 'We will have sorted through everything and if they are here we will let you know.'

What if they find more than one set of dentures — how would we recognise them? That particular search could reveal dozens lurking in festive napkins and a set of dentures could belong to anyone! It didn't bear thinking about. I covered over the very gooey cake that was looking at me from my plate. Nauseating thoughts such as I was experiencing were not conducive to eating the likes of cream horns.

End of show. The carer returned to the kitchen.

It was a slow process emptying the hall of all its visitors. Most were in wheelchairs or walking with the aid of Zimmer frames, a slow shuffle out to the waiting coaches and cars. There really was no point getting up too soon, we might as well sit for a few more minutes. Someone tapped me on the shoulder. 'Do these belong to anyone on your table?' There was one of our own Home's napkins and nestling inside was our resident's teeth. Marvellous, they couldn't possibly belong to anyone else. Suddenly the clouds lifted . . . I wrongly assumed that that person had sat at the table next to us. No, he sat two tables away from ours. How had the teeth got THERE?

Their owner hadn't moved from my side, not even to go to the toilet in the interval. We couldn't work it out and in fact never did. Were they so used to travelling around on their own that they had somehow self-propelled themselves over there? The most rational answer and only a slight possibility was that one of the waitresses had picked up the napkin while clearing the table, then, on her way to the kitchen, had stopped at another table where she had absentmindedly put them down and left them.

Just another of life's little imponderables in the Home. One of the many which surfaced from time to time. For instance, how could the night staff get a resident out of bed quickly as she needed the commode without waking and upsetting the cat which was sound asleep on top of her?

Or, how could another resident when sitting on the hoist seat of a bath submerged from the waist down, still demand to sit on a DRY seat while bathing?! No, the answer was not to cover the seat with a plastic bag. I couldn't really see that there was an answer.

And then there was: how could I get rid of all the 'blackness'— more commonly known as the night — from outside one gentleman's window. Curtains tightly closed was not the answer. As I wasn't around at the time of the Creation it was just another problem that I couldn't solve.

What about: how could I make sure that there weren't any dead bodies in the books that one of my ladies read. She was an avid reader of murder and detective novels. Murders usually produced dead bodies! The only reason I could think of as to why she had this aversion was that she was only 94 at the time and hadn't yet quite come to terms with anything dead.

Once a month, the Housebound Library Service delivered a good selection of large-print books and cassettes. The latter being of great benefit to those with impaired sight. It was an excellent service, giving freedom of choice and personal escapism for a while. Another reason to exercise their legs and their minds. Not all were interested — they no longer had the staying power or concentration needed to read a book. Others never had so they weren't going to start at that time of their lives. There was however a good clutch of avid readers and this included the respite visitors. They didn't care where they read, as long as they had a gripping novel in their hands — in the lounge during the day or in their rooms at night, uninterrupted. Sometimes they would stay in their rooms all day not wanting to be diverted for a single moment so hooked were they onto the plot of the current book.

Before the library started delivering books I would select them from the local library when requested. Although the service was good it obviously did not offer the same choice to my residents as, unless they requested specific authors, I obviously had to impose my own thoughts and preferences into the selection. In one case however, I found this beneficial as did my night staff. One lady just loved doctor and nurse romances. When selecting her books for her I could run a cursory glance over the subject matter and make sure no dire diseases or illnesses were described in detail in the book. Joyce had an overactive imagination and was also a pretty good actress! Now that she was able to select her own books how could we ensure in advance that the heroine had not got some obscure, terminal illness that the reader would imagine she had. Invariably the symptoms would appear during the night. She could start with cancer anywhere in her body, quickly followed by a heart attack or stroke. As dawn lit the sky it would be time for pneumonia to set in and then on to bronchitis, just squeezing in a sore throat before the day staff reported for duty. The only traumas she didn't experience over the years were childbirth and rabies.

'Did you have a good night Joyce?' the day carer would enquire tongue in cheek already having received the report from the departing night staff.

'Not bad, dear', would come the reply, 'just a slight tickle in the throat, but apart from that I slept well.'

The only real problem with all of that was the danger that buried in amongst the pretence was the real thing. Yes, it was a difficult problem for me to ensure there were no terrible illnesses in the hospital books for which she craved.

And the last imponderable: how is it that after 10 hours of solid work my night staff were more bright eyed and bushy tailed than was I after eight hours solid sleep?

To celebrate her change from night to daytime duties one of my staff gave the rest an impromptu floorshow of what I was like when awoken in the night for an emergency (was she implying I looked like that in the morning too?). She crawled through the doorway, on all fours, one eye tightly closed and the other twitching.

How some people exaggerate! For goodness sake I cannot even get down on my hands and knees anymore let alone walk on them! The rest of the description was fairly accurate though . . .

ATTRACTIONS
nature's remedies

'Have you ever thought what you would do if you ran out of residents?' asked a regular visitor to the Home.

'Oh!' I answered as nonchalantly as possible and clearing my throat which had suddenly become dry. 'I could possibly turn it into a hotel or bed and breakfast establishment.'

Did I ever think what would happen if we had empty rooms? He had to be joking! Well yes, I did and fairly frequently actually.

In fact, it was always the second thought that I had after a resident died. The first thoughts encompassed those of sorrow and duties to be performed, to the benefit of the newly deceased, their relatives and then to my staff. Then the second thought loomed large — 'what if I should run out of residents?'

There was mostly a healthy waiting list but as all Home owners know, waiting lists can be extremely nebulous. A prospective resident may have run out of waiting time and had to go into another Home if one could not offer a room exactly when needed, or their health may have deteriorated and had to be taken into hospital or they may even have . . . died. The list needed constant updating.

'Well,' went on the visitor jokingly, 'I was thinking as you are so close to many main cities and towns you could turn it into a bordello!'

'No,' I answered faintly, 'I haven't ever thought along those lines.' 'Right,' I said to my staff over the next few days as one by one they reported for work, 'if I turned this place into a bordello, would you stay on and do your duty?'

'No way', they all said. Or words to that effect. And very loosely translated. I was so impressed.

Sex wasn't a great problem in the Home. With the residents I mean. Not usually, anyway. From time to time a lady might fancy a member of the opposite sex but not often and usually it was the respite visitors they preferred, presumably because they went away after a week or so and wouldn't be a problem to them when their feelings went off the boil!

Sometimes ladies who always ate their breakfast in their rooms would make a terrific effort and have breakfast in the dining room with their victim, beautifully dressed, manicured and made-up. It was good to see. Interest in the opposite sex, even at a late stage, had its benefits — aches, pains and depression would all fly out of the window even if only for a short while.

Less often it would be a gentleman who made the running (or shuffling). Jack quite unashamedly said that he liked clothes and to look smart so that he could attract the ladies. He was well into his nineties by then.

A lady from a nearby village stayed for two weeks respite care and, although they had never met before, they spent every moment they could together. By the second week Jack was frequently telling her that he loved her. About a week after her departure I was in her village and decided to pop in and see how she was getting on. I had a bit of a shock I must admit because she was sitting by the fire in one of my old nightdresses (which had been put into the Home for use in emergencies). It gave me a quick insight into what I would look like in 20 or 30 (or maybe even 10) years time! All a bit depressing really. Anyway, she asked after her admirer and sent her love.

When I got home I repeated her message to him. 'Who's she?' he enquired. I explained but Jack still look mystified.

'Yes, you do know her.' I repeated her name and message. No better. 'Yes you DO. You used to tell her that you loved her.'

'Oh, THAT one. Yes, now I know who you're talking about — but I never did know her name'!

Names obviously weren't important as I found out on another occasion.

One day I invited a lady who had previously been staying for respite care to the Home for afternoon tea as it was her birthday and she lived quite alone. She spent the entire afternoon sitting beside another gentleman on a two-seater settee, chatting incessantly. When it was time to take her home I asked her friend if he would like to accompany her. Actually, we passed through the village where, many years beforehand, he had lived and he loved a ride through it at any opportunity. It had about three streetlights in its main street but Blackpool itself could not compete with those three lights in his estimation. The couple sat side by side on the back seat. When we arrived at her home she got out and as she did so she called out, 'Goodbye Charlie.'

Charlie? Who was he? Certainly not the gentleman still sitting on my back seat. I didn't even have anyone called Charlie in the Home. She had mistaken him for someone entirely different. Or had she? Was this in fact one of the benefits of old age — you could chat up any one you liked the look of and then pretend you thought they were someone else?

During the time that the Home was being enlarged one of my sons came to stay. For approximately a week our own shower room was non-operational so he used the one next door to our private flat which, at the time, was still within the Home. Unfortunately a new cleaner had started work only a few days previously and had not met any of my family. Imagine her astonishment to see a young man in his early twenties, clad only in a towel, coming out of a room — a room that she had wrongly assumed was that of one of the residents!

Fortunately this particular elderly lady loved a joke and had a pretty good sense of humour so she loved the implication — an 83 year old entertaining a toy-boy — and she dined off it for weeks.

I'm not sure that my son found it quite so amusing!

Settling new residents or respite visitors into their rooms naturally takes quite a bit of time. There is so much to explain, ask or demonstrate.

'If you wake in the night and want anything', I would ramble on, 'just ring this bell, and a lady will appear and see to your needs.' It seemed a perfectly reasonable and comforting thing to say. After a while I realised that I had to change the wording of that invitation especially if the resident was male and even more especially if accompanied by a son or son-in-law. At those words their eyes would glaze over and I could feel the younger generation doing their mental arithmetic working out how many more years to go before they could come and join us.

'Hello Dad,' said the voice on the other end of the telephone, 'how are you?'

'Very well, thank you', came the reply. Conversations had to be concise and to the point for some residents to be able to cope, with my carers or I listening in and helping to translate or shouting replies or twiddling with the hearing aid.

Or taking the telephone up to their bedroom as in this case.

'What are you doing?' continued the son. After a lot of thought came the answer.

'I've just had my tea (proceeded to go through the menu) and then I had a bath with two young ladies (well, we knew what he meant). Now I'm sitting in front of the television in my dressing gown, having a glass of whisky.'

There was an incredibly long pause from the other end. Eventually I took the receiver and asked if the son was still there and was he alright. 'No, I'm not alright', he growled. 'I'm sitting on the M25 car park going nowhere and imagining what it would be like to be in a bath with two young ladies. Right now I'd rather be 92!'

There was no answer to that.

Bath time also brought its embarrassing moments. Most of them fortunately, one-offs. The problem with a one-off is that whatever one learns from it isn't particularly beneficial because it doesn't happen again.

A lady resident was walking sedately down the stairs at the bottom of which were some glass doors leading out to a ramp and part of the garden. The carer had gone ahead carrying the toiletries and was running the bath. I was just ambling alongside her as she was very able-bodied at the time. As we turned the dogleg at the bottom of the stairs she espied one of our gentlemen residents. As quick as a flash she tore open her dressing-gown revealing a completely naked body underneath. 'Here I am, take me', she cried, with a wicked gleam in her eye. Fortunately he was already nearly blind, so missed the show and, if he hadn't been beforehand, he certainly would have been after as would anyone innocently entering through the glass doors!

One of the nicest friendships between the opposite sexes was nurtured in the garden. In a way the garden was almost divided into three or four different rooms. This meant that residents could sit outside with their visitors and family and still be reasonably private and secluded if they so wished. One part had high hedges behind which were herbaceous borders with a grass 'serpentine' path meandering between them. In this haven our lady and gentleman, Bella and Don, would often sit and, as it was summertime, they would have afternoon tea there and the lady would be 'mother'.

The day came when Bella was to attend a family wedding. My carers dressed her beautifully bringing in extra accessories of their own to co-ordinate and enhance her own outfit. She was 'made-up', her hair was set, nails manicured and all we needed to complete the picture was a corsage of flowers for the bodice. She chose from the garden those flowers that she wanted and we made them into two lovely sprays — one for the lapel and the other we attached to her clutch bag.

When dressed she regally walked down the stairs and there, waiting for her at the bottom, was her gentleman admirer. With tears in his eyes Don gently lifted her hand and kissed it and said, 'My dear, you look lovely.'

'Ooh', we all cooed.

'Aah', said our lady as she swooned. Her knees buckled and as she sank to the ground, her hand clutching the bag and flowers shot up and fused with the flowers on her coat — and there they were, splattered all over her chest!

We couldn't believe it — all that preparation for all that . . . mess! We all agreed though that it was worth it just for the look in her eyes and once we had cleaned her up she looked pretty smart again.

And then Don got ill.

And she lost interest!

Oh well, *c'est la vie*! But much better than pills while it lasted!

COMMUNICATION
who needs words?

'Is it time for bed yet?'

'No, not yet, unless you want to go early.'

'No, not particularly.'

'Why do you ask?'

'When I go to bed I get a cuddle and a goodnight kiss. I hadn't had a goodnight kiss for 66 years until I came here. I like going to bed.'

After that she got a kiss or a cuddle apropos nothing in particular and not just at bedtime.

So many forms of communication and body language. For a lot of us, speech is the most important but, when living with elderly people, one is increasingly aware that there are many more forms of it and ones which are more acceptable.

We had a lady at the Home who had been the victim of a debilitating stroke but who still had a wonderful personality with a totally lucid mind and who was deeply interested in all that went on around her. Relatively young, she coped well with her disability, solidly supported by her loving family and a special loving friend. She knew everything that was going on in her family circle and was included in all events however minor. She was indeed, still a vital part of that family and they, in turn, made sure that she knew it. However, she got so frustrated at times and never more so than when she couldn't make herself understood.

Very often I would be in the kitchen and a member of staff would come in and start to tell me what this lady had said, what she had done, where she had been (whether she enjoyed it or not), what she was doing next. After a while, I would say, 'She said all that, did she?', and we would both smile. Of course not. She could only say one word.

Being a cog in a wheel is the measure of a good carer — being part of a listening staff team who have the time and interest in a person to repeat and repeat a look or a sign until they knew what it meant and in what context. And then convey their new knowledge to the rest of the team. Writing up reports is essential, but sometimes verbal reports have the edge — one can be so much more explicit.

Having bad or little eyesight, and therefore denied eye contact or facial expressions, makes communication difficult. As does deafness. Such residents seemed to have the need, more than hearing and seeing residents, to clasp the hand — press it, grip it. They could speak to show their feelings through the fingers and grips. They could also direct the carer into the correct and best position for them to hear, speak and see.

Not everyone though, likes or can cope with the sense of touch. Some need their own space and it is essential for the staff to know that. Not this next lady though, having very little sight and very little hearing, she needed to touch and hold hands . But she did have the most brilliant memory. In her mid-nineties it was to her that I reported if I wanted to know the day and date of the week! She lived through the life of her family. She knew every club the great grandchildren attended , what they did and where they went. The staff knew the family well. It helped with their background knowledge and they too could talk about things of interest to the resident. Their voices levelled at a certain pitch, bodies in a certain position, sunlight shaded from the residents' eyes for better viewing. If all this were taken into consideration conversation could flow albeit with a certain amount of difficulty. No point talking to a deaf person with one's back to them or addressing the air over the top of their head or down at their feet. Knowing the residents was essential.

Sometimes one is bereaved of too much, too suddenly, with no time in between to fully mourn individually each passing aspect of one's own life. One gentleman came to us recently widowed and desperately missing his wife. Ill health decreed that he should sell his business. No longer able to drive and no longer able to live in his own house and moving from his roots. He tried very hard to readjust helped by the support of his daughter-in-law, family and my staff. They all tried so hard as did the medical team. He cried a lot especially when alone in his bedroom. He needed to.

'I feel so inadequate', said a carer upon finding him alone and crying. 'I couldn't think of anything to say.'

'So what did you do?'

'Nothing, I just held his hand and wept with him.'

That is not doing nothing. Sometimes gently weeping with a person is the strongest form of communication acceptable at that moment. And infinitely more comforting than saying 'I know' when the resident knows full well that you don't. That gentleman died shortly afterwards from a massive stroke — or was it a massive broken heart?

Laughter, one of the nicest forms of communication, formed a large part of our lives. Laughter with, but never at, our residents and their visitors. Giving and sharing were also important. Gifts which residents gave from time to time to their fellow residents, the sharing of sweets, drinks, the gift of listening and taking interest, the church kneeler, the tapestry performed by a resident with very little eyesight, only being able to embroider a few stitches at a time, insisting we use it for our church services. Everyone sharing the pleasure.

A gift of understanding between residents regardless of the fact they were drawn from different backgrounds. I walked into the lounge one New Year's Eve. The lights were low, the fire brightly flickering and *Die Fleidermaus* was being shown on television. Not always everyone's choice but, on this occasion, all were watching. Some residents were knitting, some sitting listening, eyes closed. Three ladies, their voices still 'true' if a little feeble, were doing a sing-along to the opera. The other ladies and gentlemen were enchanted and lifted by the music and the beauty of the lovely gowns. There was a feeling of total harmony — not bad between so many people from quite a variety of educational, financial, social and religious backgrounds. It was to end the year on a high note.

Happiness for me was walking into the lounge on a grey, colourless day and seeing all the residents united and glued to the television . . . again! What were they watching? It was the rugby World Cup final — yes really, even the ladies! In fact happiness for me was always if the residents were united. Who cared what the weather was like.

Of course the feelings in the communal lounge were not always those of total friendliness, unselfishness, or understanding of each other. Unhappiness was walking into the lounge with perhaps 11 residents present and 10 of them wanting to watch television, all different channels, or listen to tapes (again, not the same ones) and the eleventh wanting complete quiet. Why could they not watch or listen to their own programmes in the privacy of their own rooms — everyone had their own television or cassette player? No, that would have been too easy! From time to time they all needed to stamp their supremacy and identity into the lounge. And why not? They were after all normal members of the human race.

Another fun thing for the staff to have to do was to light the first fire of the winter and then have to rearrange all the seating positions, and then when the warm weather returned, change them all back again. There was plenty of communicating going on those days (and the next and the next!) After those particular exercises my staff could have gone into the Diplomatic Service. I tried to be out for those days! Everyone communicated with each other but not quite in the way we would have wished them to. But I must reiterate, considering the different personalities, interests, backgrounds and the vast amount of time spent together, they all got on very well. And what was especially nice to see was the amount of support they and their relatives gave to each other when needed. They knew how to close ranks.

Even if the more accepted forms of communication have weakened just being on the same wavelength as another person is all that is needed to make someone feel wanted and happy. No eye-contact, touch or acknowledgement of another person's presence — in fact no communication at all when in the company of at least one other person — is off-putting. In the presence of a room full of people it can be devastating.

I experienced such an occasion a year or so before opening my Home. It was at the stage when I needed to know exactly what was on the market in the shape of aids and accessories, to assist in the movement of my potential residents. Not only what one liked but in accordance with the requirements of the Fire, Environmental and Registration bodies. I asked my neighbour to accompany me to browse around one of the halls at the NEC which was staging such a show. We drove to the exhibition car park and then boarded a bus to take us to the appropriate hall. There were one or two other conferences or whatever taking place in the other halls there. Obviously all very male orientated because every other person on that bus was male. All smartly suited with briefcases on their laps. It was an odd couple of minutes. Each man an island unto himself — just staring down at his briefcase. No doubt rehearsing a speech or getting himself into the mood and the identity of the person he would have to become for the next few hours. Not a single person spoke to another.

We got off the bus and didn't say anything for a moment. Then my friend shivered and said, 'I have never experienced anything quite like that before.' And neither had I. It was not nice. It was not intended and no doubt all of those gentlemen on any other occasion would have behaved in a friendly fashion but it was this experience which helped form the basis of the welcome to the Home of the newly arrived resident. No one must ever feel lonely. It only needed one person to be welcoming for some of that fear to disappear and for the new resident to respond and so gradually be embraced into the Home.

One resident was becoming increasingly confused. This annoyed one of the ladies who tended to make rather unkind remarks to him (when she thought no one was listening).

'Why do you always fight his battles for him?' I asked another lady. This lady was one of our more timid residents and she was acting out of character. I was intrigued.

'When I first walked into the lounge', she replied, he looked up and said, "Hello my dear, I hope you will be very happy here". I shall never forget that nor how I felt on that occasion and NO ONE will ever criticise or be unkind to him in my presence.' I know it took quite a bit of doing for her to act like that. First impressions are so important. Especially when wrapped up in the communication is the gift of kindness.

Before a resident was admitted to the Home they were requested to fill in a form stating their likes and dislikes. This covered such subjects as preferred time to get up, go to bed, interests, diets, to mention but a few. One very important question was, 'By which name do you wish to be called?' Mostly that person would prefer a Christian name but sometimes it would be a nickname and very rarely as Mr or Mrs. There were only ever three collective names used — residents, ladies and gentlemen. What we didn't wish to hear them request was: 'The young can call me by my surname and the older staff by my Christian name.' When does one stop being young and whoever wanted to be classed as old? And then there were those who thought (being 90 plus) that anyone under 60 was young! Never mind it usually sorted itself out. Calling a person by the name that they wish to be called was of the utmost importance. To call them anything else would be rude. In the important matter of communication it would be wide of the desired mark.

Happy vibes, good communication, shared interests and friendship. Why is there always an adverse side of the coin? One lady, already bereaved in several areas, found friendship again in the Home. Unfortunately it could not last for long as the friend died a year or so later. Another good friendship was cemented and that too was brought to an end within the year for the same reason. And again, for a third time, the same outcome.

'That's it', she said. 'No more friendship, I cannot cope with the sadness and the sense of loss.' She kept her word and we could not persuade her otherwise. She made no more good friends and kept herself to herself. She was adamant she would not change her mind. From that time on her health deteriorated and she started on a slow downward spiral — and she really didn't care. Her friends had kept her going for a few more years but, sadly, she had outlived them all and now had lost the willpower to continue.

Time and time again we found that as long as we did the mundane, basic, everyday slog, the fine tuning would be implemented for us out of the blue — but only after we had discussed and worked *ad nauseum* at ways and means of overcoming the current problem. And it wasn't always the most experienced carer involved in those discussions who put those words into action — it worked on every level and in every age group. As long as someone was in the right place at the right time and trying hard.

A lady came to stay with us for several weeks after having had a mental breakdown. Although helped by medication and attended to by the medical profession at the hospital it became clear that Muriel could not continue to live on her own for a while. So a close friend of hers persuaded her to accept respite care until well enough to return home. Initially she could not bear to venture out of her room, staying there all day even for mealtimes. Slowly the medication working she became stronger and more confident once again realising the need for company. But no matter how she tried, initially Muriel could not pluck up the courage to enter the lounge, so one or two residents, if invited, would visit her in her room — gradually breaking down barriers.

Working at the Home at the time was a young girl, Laura, on work experience from college — one of four or five young girls with natural caring instincts who came into the Home and progressed into excellent adult carers. The residents loved her as she was always so cheerful and had an outgoing personality. In the room next to our respite resident was a registered blind gentleman. Laura loved to go in and chat with him and in the course of conversation he mentioned that he used to play the piano and had an electric organ at home. The next time that Laura reported for work, she brought with her a small keyboard — it would not take up much space in his room and would give him added pleasure and interest. Unfortunately one of the keys did not work as well as it should, so her cousin, one of our full-time carers, said she would bring in her son's keyboard which was a bit bigger. So much pleasure did this give our gentleman that, after changing the furniture around in his room, we found that there would actually be room for his own music centre and his daughter duly brought it in for him.

In the meantime while taking delivery of the three different instruments he was quietly playing away to himself, the tunes gently flowing into his neighbour's room. Soon, drawn by the music, Muriel found the confidence to go into his room. She could cope with this because he could not actually see her. For weeks they would sit and talk or he would play the piano and all the time her confidence growing. His room was between hers and the lounge. By taking one step at a time she finally made it into the lounge enjoying the company of other residents and one lady in particular with whom she would attack the crossword every morning.

It all just happened! But it took one teenage girl with interest and keenness to start the ball rolling — not just for the gentleman but for Muriel too. We had tried hard to ease the problems with both of these people but it needed not only the keyboard but also the fact that the gentleman was blind, his proximity to the lounge and for the encouragement of all the other carers to bring about the happy conclusion. Everyone was in the right place at the right time. Soon after Muriel left to return home and to continue living on her own — just as she had previously done.

Millie was another lady who was in the right place at the right time, occupying a room opposite a new lady, a foreigner by birth. By chance Millie wanted to extend her repertoire of her new neighbour's native language. 'Could you show our new lady around and direct her if you should find her wandering around lost?' I asked. 'Yes of course and while we are at it maybe she could teach me some new words.' Which she did. Both were in their early nineties! Millie had made the new lady feel welcome and needed in her first few days.

We never knew what form communication would take — knitting, music, foreign language. What did it matter, as long as the barriers came down?

Without a doubt, the most important lines of communication are between residents and loved ones — more than anyone else these the people they wanted to see. If it were not possible for the relations to pay regular visits then a telephone call or letter keeps the lines open. If the resident is hard of hearing then a letter is a joy or, for the partially sighted, a postcard bright and clear with strong outlines is much appreciated. A postcard, even for the forgetful and confused, can bring happiness because it can be shown by a carer time and time again — happiness for the actual moment is of optimum importance. The more there are of such moments, the happier the Home.

Knowledge of a resident's needs is never more important than when they are close to death. Their means of communication at a minimum — eye contact and touch — are even more important. Little things, like knowing how many pillows a resident likes and at what angle they should be placed, is important. Bearing in mind that regular turning is essential at that time it is still important to bring in the maximum amount of comfort and normality into their lives. The mouthwashes, face cooling, gentle creaming, attention to pressure areas and talking to them about their family and interests. Even if they cannot reply they can often still hear. And they still have feelings. It brings them a feeling of security at an insecure time and knowledge that their needs and wants will be carried out without any words being uttered.

Staff frequently stayed on well after their shift had finished, sitting beside the resident, holding their hand, relieving the family for a while and knowing full well that the resident would not be there the next time they were on duty.

In a lot of cases, it also meant that they would not see a dear friend again.

HOLY COMMUNION

And so to the highest level of communication. 11.00 am Holy Communion — alternate Tuesdays in the lounge. A fairly straightforward, innocuous statement, you would think. Not so! There was nothing straightforward about our Holy Communion services. In fact, the service held in our lounge once a fortnight was unlike any service I had ever attended in Church.

I can only liken it to an old television game show of many years ago — Chinese puzzles. The contestants were presented with about a dozen canes, onto the top of which, one by one, were placed breakable plates which were then kept spinning at great speed to ensure they did not crash to the floor. The winner was the contestant who controlled the largest number of spinning plates. In order to keep them aloft, they had to rush frantically from one cane to another giving each another wobble to continue the spinning before hurtling off to the next — hence keeping the plates balanced and in their rightful places.

And then, just when they thought all were under control, one would start to wobble off.

On alternative Tuesdays mornings I was that contestant. Our local vicar or his curate would arrive just before 11.00 for a service that lasted between 20 and 30 minutes. Longer if too many plates wobbled off their canes! This was followed by the vicar taking Communion to any resident who requested it in their room before having a general chat with the other ladies and gentlemen. All were welcome to the service with visitors to the Home joining us.

Our vicar's mother had, for a short time, been one of our residents, so he and his wife and family knew the Home more intimately than a lot of the visitors. Most of the residents were known to him personally especially those who had lived in the village. The family had witnessed the basic, everyday slog of the running of the Home. They understood the problems, upsets, joys and pain and at other times, joined in with the fun and laughter.

Our Communion service was a joy to our vicar, curate and myself and there was complete understanding and complete respect for all the participants. Understanding that even if the 'spirit is willing' the body literally does not always have the staying power! The Home provided the physical, mental and emotional care and the Churches completed the picture looking after the spiritual needs for all denominations.

It was a busy time just before the service with furniture to be rearranged, the coffee table to be adapted into an 'altar', the vicar's kneeler to be put in place and coffee cups to be collected. Carers took all those who wished for a last visit to the toilet, made sure all were sitting comfortably with foot stalls in place and escorted any stragglers from their bedrooms to the lounge. Then lastly, take anyone who didn't wish to attend either to their rooms or to the kitchen where they could sit and chat to the carers and cook.

Most weeks there were usually 12 to 13 communicants including myself. Apart from anything else I had to be there to scoop anyone up off the floor should the situation arise.

The service started well in that the vicar walked in correctly garbed and greeted everyone. I wouldn't say that from then on it was downhill all the way because it certainly wasn't but variations to the normal course of events crept into the service. Three residents would look up, get up and 'zimmer' off to the toilets (just in case). They only went five minutes ago so they didn't really need to go at all. While waiting for their return I would give out the order of service sheets. Two residents eventually came back but not the third. He was having difficulties and needed assistance and would no doubt return sometime during the middle of the service.

'I've got the wrong glasses', says another resident. 'These are for distance and I need my reading ones.'

I rush up to her bedroom. No, not in her bedside drawer and not visible on any surface but luckily I spy them peeping out the top of her denture mug.

Back to the lounge passing the third resident and carer on the way. We all settle down, all eyes on the vicar. There is a nudge from my neighbour.

'I haven't got my teeth in', in a loud stage whisper.

'You won't need them', I loudly whisper back not wanting to prolong the start any longer.

'How can I eat the bread?'

'Did you have them in for breakfast?'

'Yes!'

'Well, you haven't been anywhere so you must still have them.'

I do a rapid search. Not in her handbag. Not in her rolled-up handkerchief but best not to look to closely into that!

Gingerly I put my fingers down the side of the chair. No teeth.

'I've just remembered', she says, 'I didn't put them in this morning.'

'Well you ate your cereals and two pieces of toast so a small round of wafer bread should not prove too difficult.' I get a 'look' which withers me and I fade away back to my seat and the service.

From time to time our local dentist would call on the residents at the Home to correct ill-fitting dentures and attend to other problems of the mouth. This sometimes meant that he had to take their teeth back to the surgery to work on them with the specialised equipment.

'How will I eat?', they cry.

'Don't worry, we will give you suitable food, I soothingly reply.

This is too easy an answer and not dramatic enough and anyway, they don't want to give up their toffees and biscuits etc. Not even for a day. The dentist has heard all this before.

'You'll just have to do what everyone else without teeth does', he cheerily replies. 'Gum it to death'.

She gummed her circle of bread when the time came.

Right, we were ready to carry on with (or even start) our service. Unfortunately, while all this has been going on the sun has now burst through the clouds and through the large patio windows enveloping half of the residents in a massive sunbeam. The warmth from this has at least one lady slumped sideways in her chair in an instant, sound asleep. I rush over to her and prod her gently awake, turn round to find the resident with whom I was sharing the two seater sofa, leaning heavily over to my side also about to nod off. I approach the sofa, gyrate my body onto the seat and upwards, beaming her body up as I go and at last both she and I are upright.

And so we continue with the service. Eyes firmly closed and hands clasped. Who needs teeth and glasses for the Lord's Prayer as they recite the familiar and much loved words? Even residents who cannot talk properly or some who on a bad day could not even remember what the word prayer meant repeat the familiar words as if miraculously they have no speech or memory problems. They are safe and secure in the knowledge and power of God's love.

But why, I ask myself, if we all start praying at the same time, on the same word, is there always one person who is always two words in front of the rest of us — or two words behind? They don't progressively get quicker or slower so it cannot be put down to bad hearing or bad sight. If it were so, they should by the time we have finished that particular prayer, be two or three lines in front — or behind. Fortunately, I have never had a 'slow' and a 'quick' resident in the Home at the same time, otherwise presumably, it would take three times as long to get through the service. And why is it always the ladies who have this tendency?

Which brings me to another question. If on hairdressing mornings one of our residents would refuse to take her water pill because she did not want to keep getting out from under the dryer (or even worse lose her place in the mythical queue) why did she quite happily take it on Communion morning? After all, it had the same effect on her every morning of the week. Could it be that she was . . . a female?!

But we move on — on to the Creed. This should present no difficulties. All they have to do is sit there and again, repeat well known sentences. I also sit, head bowed, one eye open. I spend the whole service actually with one eye open, both literally and metaphorically, to ensure that every one is alright. Suddenly, to my horror, I see the pair of knees opposite to me starting to move up and down. 'Please God don't let her kneel. If this lady forgets she cannot kneel and kneels down it will take the hoist to get her up again', I think to myself. By now I have reluctantly abandoned the Creed and am engaged in a mental exercise rearranging seats, stools, altar and residents, so a hoist, should it be needed, could gain entrance. It would cause chaos and pandemonium.

'Please, please God don't let her kneel!'

He answered my prayers. Someone was passing behind the vicar's back and merrily waving. Quite oblivious to what was going on in the lounge our part time gardener was walking past the patio doors in the garden. He was everyone's friend. The knees' attention was taken!

'Who's that?' asked someone in a totally normal voice not even attempting to whisper.

'It's the gardener', came a chorus of replies.

'Oh, is it Wednesday?'

'No, I don't think so.'

'What is he doing outside?'

'I said he's the gardener.' But the knees had shuffled back to their rightful place and position on the chair.

Arms which had not been raised so high since keep fit the previous Thursday were waving. The vicar could not see him – after all he had his back to the window.

How could they POSSIBLY see him? They were all wearing their reading glasses and in most cases would not have been able to see much further than their toes. By now the Creed was finished and my residents carried on the service as if nothing had happened.

But now I was finding it hard not to giggle. We were getting there. The vicar had reached the stage when he called us to the General Confession. Once more our eyes were closed and our heads bowed. All was silent except for a shuffling noise.

One of those plates was about to wobble off. Yes, it was my water-logged, tableted resident needing to excuse herself. She shuffled off to the door — a heavy, fire safety door — which she had no chance of opening on her own, getting herself and her walking frame through at the same time and out into the passage way. Why did I try to look unobtrusive as I got up to help her? There was really no point. Everyone was watching anyway.

On my way back I meet the third absconding resident who was now ready to rejoin us and accompany him to the lounge. Good — just in time for the Prayer of Absolution. Pity really, under the circumstances I hadn't been present to actually confess my sins.

The responses the vicar receives from his communicants upon receiving the Bread and Wine are many and varied. And not strictly from the prayer book but it doesn't matter — it still means the same. They include: 'Thank you', 'Amen', 'Can I have a bit more?', 'Thank you my dear', and 'That's a drop of good' — the last accompanied by the smacking of the recipient's lips (after the wine, of course). It has even been known for the vicar to have to wrestle the Chalice away from the odd pair of lips! On that particular day however, my fellow sofa sharer said, 'Thank you Victor'. No, not 'Victor', the name should have come out as 'vicar', but her teeth got in the way. Once again I could feel the laughter bubbling to the surface. Please God you helped me earlier in the service, please do so again now.

Not many days beforehand one of my residents had died. Jane had been with me for many years and we were close friends. Just prior to her death she had had stroke after stroke and her quality of life soaked away day by day. With her loving and supportive family by her side and her loving and supportive carers tending to her every need, she gently died.

It is so easy to tell oneself that it was what she would have wanted and what was right for her. The trouble with bereavement is that just when you are beginning to feel emotionally strong again something small and trivial leaps out at you and there your are, back at square one again. That is what 'Victor' did to me.

Jane must have attended easily 150 such services with me over the years (or variation on the same theme as this service), and usually sat opposite me. If someone needed attention she would direct me to them with her eyes. If something untoward occurred I would look up and meet her eyes — filled with concern or amusement or whatever. But this time when I looked up to smile Jane wasn't there and the inner laughter turned to inner tears.

The Service was over. The vicar having visited the room communicants, had a coffee and freshly baked cake from the kitchen and then we said our 'goodbyes' and 'thank yous'

I went back into the lounge. 'Could you get me a cardigan from my room please?' asked my toothless resident. 'Certainly.' I ran up the stairs, walked into her bedroom and smiled back at her teeth which were smiling at me from behind a bowl of hyacinths. It was, after all, a very normal day!

WHY RESPITE?

'Hello,' she called walking towards me with a smile on her face. 'Hel-lo,' I answered hesitantly, not quite sure who she was.

'You remember me, don't you?', she laughed.

'Yes', I lied also laughing.

'No you don't, I can tell you don't'.

So much for my acting prowess!

'No, I don't', I admitted.

'Well you should, you saw me a mere hour and a half ago'.

Recognition and realisation dawned. This was the daughter of an old gentleman whom I'd collected to take to a day centre. I had talked to her at 9.00 am when I picked him up as usual and as usual she had been pleasant in a quiet sort of way and soberly dressed.

Now however, a transformation had taken place. So much so that I genuinely had not recognised her as that same daughter. No only was she well made-up but her body language shouted out, 'I'm free'. She was metaphorically skipping along the street. 'Oh, yes', she laughed, 'this is my time to myself. I look after my father all week, day and night.

I love him very much, he is a lovely gentleman and really appreciates it but on Fridays from 9.00 am-3.00 pm I do whatever I want. This morning I've had my hair done and am meeting friends for coffee. I often do this but not always. Sometimes I read a book all day or take my breakfast back to bed and then go back to sleep. Or my friends and I go out to lunch. Whatever I feel like doing, I do and that way I don't resent the rest of the week.'

That conversation took place probably 10 years before I opened my Home but the impact that it made on me at the time was considerable. And that was when the seed of knowledge of the importance of respite care was initially sown.

Most of the time I had either one or two respite beds. Sometimes these would be extended to three when, after the death of a resident, the room would remain empty until the next resident was ready to come in. This was sometimes two or three weeks and it served a useful purpose if there was someone desperate for a week's holiday.

Why 'respite' and who benefited?

The word 'respite' means a temporary cessation, pause, interval or rest etc and anyone looking after their elderly relation or a disabled spouse knows the importance of this. As indeed does anyone living on their own and wanting to remain doing so but at the same time longing for a break in the everyday struggle — a time to renew energies.

Most of our respite visitors either lived with, adjacent to, or near their families. Their chief carers being a daughter or daughter-in-law and backed up by the husband and in some cases grandchildren and Social Services. While the elderly person remained relatively fit the system worked quite well. It was when they moved into the grey area between coping and not coping (or indeed coping and not realising they were not coping) that the pressures upon the carers mounted up.

The fear that their parent had fallen, not taken their medication, wandered off, allowed a stranger into the home, boiled saucepans dry, given away something of value to someone they scarcely knew and so on. Frequently ringing the family day and night.

Panic buttons are an excellent idea but if a person doesn't fall near one it is of no use. The kind worn around the neck is an equally excellent idea — they have saved hundreds of lives — as long as the wearer remembers to put it on. The list is interminable — no doubt each carer having their personal bad experience to add to that list.

Elderly parents who couldn't cope generated carers who could never switch off. Never again able to go out without clock watching — just in case. Rushing back to serve the next meal, worried they would be delayed somewhere along the line. When the going got hard Social Services stepped in with their Care in the Community plans — getting up, dressing, administering medication, putting to bed and midday meals from the Meals on Wheels service. It took the pressure off the carers and was invaluable if the elderly person did not have personal carers of their own, as in many cases the family lived many miles away.

What about the hours in between and the nights? The constant telephone calls, the hospital visits, optician, dentist, clinic and surgeries? Then as well as the house there was the garden to keep under control. A carer who retained a lot of the personal caring, even with backup, still had that extra layer of pressure apart from their own personal life with which to cope.

A few months before my mother died she came to live with us. One day in the middle of winter the ground covered with a thick layer of snow, I was attacked by a dog whilst out walking my own dog. Its teeth marginally missing the jugular vein but creating quite a nasty wound.

Returning home as quickly as my wobbly legs would allow I checked that my mother was alright. She was fast asleep. No need to wake her and worry her knowing I would not be too long as the local surgery had agreed that I could go there rather than go several miles to the hospital. In a state of shock I drove myself there.

The procedure took longer than I had anticipated in my ignorance and it was a while before I returned home. My mother, far from being worried, was in fact very annoyed that I had kept her waiting an extra hour longer for her lunch! The worrying came later. Could this be my mother speaking? She who loved my brother and I so much that she would have willingly laid down her life for us. Only worried about herself? This was not my mother as she used to be.

Many carers over the years have said to me, 'you cannot imagine what it is like never being able to relax and switch off'. Well yes, I could to a certain extent because although the bite was of importance, over the following weeks that memory faded into insignificance compared with the new problems which emitted from it — that of my mother never wanting to be left alone for long.

In future I did my shopping when my neighbours were at home. Then I no longer dog walked with them but on my own so they would be on the end of the telephone if my mother should need them. Always having contingency plans for when I was away from the house. Yes, I had an inkling of what they were talking and could sympathise.

Something happens to the elderly as they become more housebound and chair bound. Loving parents who would not intentionally cause their children pain or worry become more and more inward looking and more insular. They become more insecure and need to know their carer is on the end of a buzzer or telephone. They need to know that they are safe otherwise who will pay their bills, take them to their appointments, organise them? The more they think and worry the more irrational they become and, in some cases, more physically ill.

But those carers in the community looking after their parents are often elderly themselves and they need respite. Also, with their dependants safely in a Home they can relax and rebuild their own strengths. Some would pay privately for their parent to have respite care on a regular basis, ie. one week each month or whatever. Social Services would fund a certain number of weeks a year for those in great need and not able to finance the stay themselves.

These were weeks when the carers could come and go as they pleased. Get up as late or go to bed as early as they pleased. Watch a television programme through to its ending without interruption. They could entertain friends or use that time to decorate.

Some of our regular respite users still lived alone in their own houses, supported by carers in the community but restricted in their movements by stroke related disabilities, blindness etc and unable to go out unescorted. These people could come in to recharge their batteries, meet old friends, be waited upon and be part of the general hustle and bustle of the Home. They went home revitalised and able to cope for a few more months in the homes they loved.

Other incumbents of our respite beds, although over 60 years of age, came from a younger generation. They were the ones who had just come out of hospital after a minor operation who did not need nursing but required support — even if it was only with dressing and washing. Helping them to get stronger and gain confidence to go back after a week or so to their own homes.

One of the most important aspects of respite care was that it introduced a residential lifestyle to elderly people in a gradual and more acceptable way.

I know that some would refuse to even entertain the idea, even for only a week or so or book up and then recover from the current problem and naturally feel no need to stay with us — but they were a small proportion. The beauty of short stay is that one can 'test the waters' before having to jump in feet first. The 'respiters' get to know the Home's pattern of life, its staff, layouts of rooms, menus and the next time they arrive they do not have quite as big a fear of the unknown to over-come.

When living full-time in a Home it is easy for a resident to forget the amount of support they are receiving. Gradually they feel better, safer and are oblivious of the fact that all their meals are prepared and served to them, laundry attended to, no shopping required, are bathed and put to bed and then got up again the next morning. They feel better, so much so that they are ready to go home again! Go home, in most cases to stairs that they cannot safely climb, steps they cannot step over and shops a car drive away. No grab rails, no hoist to lower them into the bath and no carers to dry those parts of their bodies they can no longer reach. The list is interminable. Forgetting how bad life was on their own fades into oblivion.

This did not tend to happen to residents who came into the Home through the gradual process of a series of respite weeks. While resting they would feel a lot better, then go home and be fine for a while and then the reality of the situa-tion — their own and their environmental limitations — would dawn on them and they would be happy to return. For those fully residential ladies and gentlemen who found it hard to settle, a week or so back at home could have soon convinced them that they were no longer able to cope alone. But for them to go back, even for a couple of weeks, would be too difficult, too dangerous and in some cases, too cruel.

In latter years three-quarters of the residents had been respite visitors, building up the time they spent with us as their disabilities increased until they arrived at the stage when they would ask to be added to the waiting list. Often they would get to the top before they were fully ready to commit themselves and would therefore remain there, sometimes rejecting several available rooms until they felt totally ready. But they had the option.

And then one day there were there. And it was good. They knew the house inside out and we knew them pretty intimately too. We knew their needs, interests, family, social background, likes and dislikes, physical, emotional and in some cases mental problems, and therefore the transition was all so much easier.

A new face, someone else to talk to, a layer of different visitors. In a residential Home where the 'turnover' was not great respite visitors on the whole were beneficial to the full-time residents. New friendships were often forged on these occasions, new interests, attitudes, ideas, gossip and a feeling of happy anticipation at the thought of future visits. Different residents brought with them different problems. New problems gave the staff a new insight into remedies and ways of overcoming them and therefore widened their experiences.

Not everyone settled in well even if in for only a week. A week can seem a lifetime if you're afraid. And not all full-time residents welcomed the newcomers. Sometimes they found they disrupted their own routine although once the carers were aware of the problems they worked at them until, hopefully, they were resolved with understanding on all sides.

The most adverse effect that respite visitors had upon our residents though, was not so easy to rectify. Our younger residents would see someone come to stay with problems very similar to their own — and yet they still lived on their own, in their own homes. How could they? It just didn't seem fair! It made them feel restless although not realising the different set of circumstances and backup such visitors received when at home. It could induce feelings of resentment towards their own families not understanding (or not wishing to understand) the frailties and impossibilities of their own personal situations.

Which brings me to elderly spouses caring for equally elderly husbands or wives. No let-up, day or night, with themselves imprisoned in their own homes, not to mention their own bodies through walking or other physical difficulties. No longer able to drive the car. Their own friends also very elderly and no longer having the opportunities to visit and help. Just taking the more dependent half of the couple into care for a week or two gives the carer respite even though not going anywhere and just relaxing in their own homes. Sadly, so often, they hate their loved one going away and feel they have let them down but if they want to stay together it is of paramount importance that they have the time to gird themselves up for the future demands. The importance of the respite which the visitor has fades into insignificance compared with the benefits that the carer will have received, with responsibilities being removed for a short while.

There was yet another facet to short-stay benefits ie. marketing. From the owner/manager's point of view it was the most effective source of advertisement. Respite residents returned back to their own town or village as did all their visitors. Word of mouth was so much more effective than the written impersonal word of a brochure. The converse side of that particular coin was that a full-time bed, on the whole, was filled for a longer period with less paperwork etc than a respite bed. If a respite visitor were to be taken ill or die just prior to their stay, it was often difficult to fill that room immediately, just for a few days.

But, on the whole, respite worked very well. Respite visitors were our 'breaths of fresh air'. They made it impossible for us to stagnate.

Very often respite visitors were not visited a great deal by their main carer — friends and lesser carers would fill this gap. After all, if the main carer spent a lot of time visiting the Home what benefit would the respite have been to them?

However, one lady respite visitor did not want anyone else to visit, only her husband. He came about twice a week although she wanted more. He lived nine or ten miles away which for him it was quite a long journey as he was well into his 80s himself. Unfortunately it was winter when she was with us. He would come out of the freezing cold into our very warm Home and immediately fall asleep. She got distraught every time he did this, prodding and poking him, trying to wake him up. In spite of the staff joining in and tempting him with food and drinks he slept long and soundly up until it was time for him to go again.

She was with us for Christmas so her husband spent the day with us too — or part of it — arriving just before lunch and then afterwards (like everyone else) nodding off to sleep. A lot of the residents went to their families for the day but there were usually five or six left plus the extra visitors and staff on duty (and sometimes their families) making a nice cosy number arranged around the fire. It seemed a good idea to play some old-fashioned games. The sister of one of our residents had previously offered to organise 'pass the parcel', 'consequences' and 'charades' (we didn't bother with 'sardines').

After about four rounds had been correctly guessed, I turned to the husband who was nodding away amicably and said, 'would you like a go now?'

'Yes please', he answered, terribly enthusiastically, whereupon he leapt to his feet. We were amazed. Never before had we witnessed such activity from him. He stood up and collected his coat and hat. Very slowly he put them on while, like a lot of idiots, we all made wild suggestions as to what he was enacting. Fully buttoned-up with scarf, hat and gloves in position, he raised his hat.

'Good-bye and thank you so much for having me'.

He thought I had said, 'would you like to go now?'. It must have been the wine slurring my speech!

THAT'S ENTERTAINMENT!

'Come to tea!' Magical words.

Every so often the sister of a resident would sing out those words — usually just after Christmas or in the summer when her garden was ablaze with colour from the beds of annuals.

It was an invitation to which we all looked forward. The residents loved her house with its beautiful antiques and it was another excuse to get really dressed up. Best clothes and a full make-up to attend that party. The brother acted as host sitting at the head of the table, loving the occasion and being able to share with his friends at the Home.

The house was on the outskirts of the village. Not far to go so a minimum of cars was needed. It was close enough for me to do a repeat drive if necessary — which often happened.

Two carers accompanied me from the Home to help with the residents. At the house there were two more mutual friends of both the sister and myself who very kindly assisted with the food etc. They knew the residents intimately which made life easier. Sometimes another friend attended to play the piano for background music or for a sing-song afterwards.

The table groaned under the weight of the food. The preparation for it must have taken ages. Table and Christmas decorations enhancing the scene.

Inevitably there were platefuls of luscious food left over. The sister was so generous in every way. On the whole, elderly people eat very little at a time and it is often difficult for other age groups to appreciate this. Rather than have all that food wasted the mutual friends would pack it up for us to take home for supper or tea the next day.

Not wishing to walk through the lounge to their cars clutching the loot, my two carers opted to go out through the back door. By now it was pitch dark and they did not immediately realise that there was a tractor parked on the doorstep. In order to get to their cars they had to squeeze themselves through the tractor, across the lawn and over a small mesh fence and onto the driveway. It was a bit like 'jeux sans frontiers' only played in the dark!

Out came the first carer clutching her bag and found to her surprise the tractor and fence but eventually managed to grope her way, grazed and shaken, to her car and then returned to the house. I was then required to take someone home who was feeling tired so I backed my car down the drive which resembled an obstacle course, unfortunately removing all the supports to the fence and burying it in the lawn.

Some time later, the second carer emerged, crawled through the tractor, tripped over the mesh and dropped her sausage rolls and mince pies all over the lawn then, much battered, she too returned to the house.

Out came the first carer again, negotiated the tractor quite well, being well practised by then but, unfortunately, the fence wasn't where it had been before. Added to that, the greasy crumbs now scattered over the lawn caused her to slip, throwing her sideways at a tangent and activating the alarm system.

A wonderful party, but so much easier to go home in the light!

It was another year, another fabulous party. The food, decorations, entertainment, excitement all as before. Crackers as usual. Mine revealed a corkscrew. Having unwrapped it but needing both hands free, I put it into a side pocket of my skirt so that I would not forget to take it home. And promptly forgot it. Until it was time to go home!

Later on I swung into the driving seat and upon making contact with the corkscrew was rapidly spiralled upwards until the top of my head slammed into the roof reducing the length of my neck by several centimetres. During that night I was awakened by the night staff requesting me to assist with residents who had over-indulged at the party. It was taking two people to keep one resident upright in the bathroom and I was needed to anchor another in the toilet. Pounding along the passageway I failed to notice that the door in front of me was shut — well it was the middle of the night — and I ran full tilt into it banging my forehead, squashing my nose and stubbing my toes! Add to all that a throbbing area, situated halfway between the head and the toes caused by the close encounter with the corkscrew and it was quite difficult making the obligatory soothing noises to the sick.

Over the years the pattern and length of outings changed especially after 'Care in the Community' came into being. Once this was operating, elderly people tended to stay longer in their own homes with the backup of the community and social services teams. In most cases quite rightly. It meant therefore, that those residents going into a residential home were older than had previously been the case. Those with bad physical disablement or confusion still needed to be accommodated whatever their age but, on the whole, pre-Community Care, the average age in our Home was

70+ to 80+, whereas after, it was 80+ to 90+. Ten years makes a big difference at that time of life — inevitably the body has become more worn out, more feeble, more frail and the downward spiral may develop into a gallop. Sleep patterns change and the cat-nap comes into its own.

So the days out — longer journeys, evening outings on the whole changed to afternoons out, shorter journeys and entertaining more within the lounge. Even if a resident was certain that he/she wanted to go on an outing when it came to it, they wouldn't want to know — they just wanted to stay safe and sound in the Home as the hassle of getting in and out of the car was too much bother.

Of course there were exceptions to every rule, even when those rules apply to nonagenarians. And to one in particular — Daphne. 'I want a ride on the dodgems. Bring me back later.' We could hardly believe our ears. Could this be our 92 (going on 10) year old? Take her back that night! She would have been trampled underfoot in the crush and melee which the 'Mop Fair' attracted as virtually everyone in the surrounding area flocked into the town for the event.

That was why we were there just before lunch. Serenely wheeling chairs easily along the roads which weren't normally free from traffic. Visiting the site of the hog-roast, watching the rides and stalls being assembled. Window shopping. Having the usual coffee or whatever in the road-side cafe.

It was difficult enough getting staff to be on duty for that one night of the year — everyone wanted to go, whether they had children or grandchildren or not! It was when one met friends and acquaintances who had not been seen since the last 'Mop'. I certainly could not raise two or three extra carers to winkle Daphne in and out of dodgems, death-defying rides and keep her in an upright position.

Daphne sulked for days. She wanted to whirl in a circle, turning round and round and up and down as she went. She loved living dangerously. She sulked for days when she found that she wasn't invited to one of my staff's hen party. It wouldn't have mattered how late it finished — or if it finished at all.

In her youth Daphne had an open-roofed sports car in which she roared around the country lanes. As she grew older she became, as did so many of my residents, chairman of this, president of that and chief organiser of so many village functions.

By day she sat in her room, talking book cassettes plugged into her ears, dead-pan expression on her face, showing no emotion as she spied, detected, assassinated, tortured and murdered. Under her skin she lived dangerously — getting through three or four cassettes a week. If she lived to be 100, I promised her a parachute jump. Well, she didn't quite get there. And although we deeply mourned her I wasn't sure if I was sorry or relieved that she didn't make that jump.

One of the best outings entailed all the residents being taken to a large venue where there was a carousel, Christmas tea, comedians, entertainment and a tea dance. Nearly all the staff wanted to go so it developed into a Christmas outing. I think the event catered for about 600 people at one sitting.

The residents were entitled to one ride each on the carousel. Many obviously did not wish to know but were very happy chatting and people-watching. A few did, sitting astride the horse (or side saddle) supported by a carer.

One ride each? Not Daphne — she had two or three. It took three helpers to lift her up and on and then to stay with her. She was in seventh heaven as round and round and up and down they went.

The afternoon ended with a tea dance. Again, some residents danced with members of staff while others were content to watch and remember. Not this lady. It took a carer either side and one facing her, arms entwined to keep her upright. Dance after dance she had. My carers were exhausted but not the nonagenarian! 'Look at her face', we all said. It wore an expression of sheer, undiluted joy. In fact there were several of us there having a little weep just looking at her.

The next day a member of staff said, 'Wouldn't it have been awful if she'd died from over-excitement on the dance floor.' No, it would have been wonderful. What a way to go! Totally happy, sublime and doing things she hadn't done for years.

It wouldn't of course, have been much fun for the other 599 people out for their Christmas party!

Did I say she was riddled with arthritis, in pain, couldn't move unaided, with very little sight and was registered blind?

We all get bombarded with junk mail. When sorting the post, one day, I saw one addressed to another great lady, also, well into her 90s. Across the front of the envelope were stamped the words "train now, if you want to be an astronaut". Well, I knew she wouldn't be interested. But I bet I knew a lady who would!

THE GARDEN
sensory pleasures

The garden was an important asset to the Home. Approximately one acre in size, we used it as often as possible and as an extension to the house.

Prior to starting the Home I had what I thought was the brilliant idea of creating a scented garden for any potential blind and partially-sighted residents. To this end I bought dozens of boxes of camomile to plant in place of one of the lawns. This was to be bordered on one side by a rose arbour cascading down either side of a south-facing bench, the highly scented flowers mingling in with more rose bushes planted nearby. That at least was the theory and I suppose, in practise, it came into being but like a lot of my 'brilliant' ideas was very short-lived. The camomile grew knotted and long and was hard to walk over and the roses had lethal thorns. It would have been dangerous enough for a fit, upright, clear-sighted person to enter such an area but to let my residents loose in it would have been disastrous — we would have had to organise a search party! So the camomile was dug up again and I re-seeded the area back to lawn. I kept the roses well tied back and many of my residents enjoyed sitting in the bower with faces uplifted to the sun soaking up the vitamins.

Although it was used mostly for pleasure the garden played a huge part in the general wellbeing of the residents. A walk around the perimeter path, well wrapped-up against the January or February weather, seeking out the first snowdrop or aconite was stimulating not only in interest but for appetite and exercise too. It was another excuse to get them to exercise their limbs. Even sitting in a wheelchair while going around the garden entailed walking or transferring to it, lifting arms to put on coat sleeves, lifting legs up to the 'supports' — all extra and beneficial — rather than just sitting. An escorted walk with the aid of a stick, frame, or carer's arm was of even greater benefit.

Out of the Home, down the ramp, past the malus, prunus, rose arbour and along to the wooded area, heavily planted with bluebells, lilly of the valley, heathers and primroses. Turn left at the car park and under the walkway of tamarix with its fronds brushing the cheeks and into the 'hidden garden' (as one lady always called it). There they could meander between the herbaceous borders before leaving through the archways of evergreens. Then up and under the pergola, past the weeping cherry and the golden maple (planted to mark the spot where our beautiful golden retriever was buried), past the potting sheds, the wygelia, rowan, honeysuckles and numerous more borders. Stop at last in front of the lounge windows there to wave at fellow residents and enter the Home again or, in the appropriate season, sit on the patio amongst the flower tubs, hanging baskets and rockery . . . or turn around and do it all in reverse! Suitably dressed they followed the seasons around finding pleasure in whatever was on show.

Chairs and benches were arranged around the garden. Residents, visitors and carers could sit, rest and chat — another important one to one session could evolve. Another opportunity to make the resident feel 'top of the pile'.

Flowers were gathered for arrangements and greenery picked to enhance bunches given as presents. One or two (mostly respite residents) sketched in the garden but in general it was mostly used for just sitting.

This was when the garden excelled itself. The patio became an extension of the lounge and often sunny, warm afternoons turned into mini-garden parties. At the beginning of the season residents were keen to sit outside. As the season wore on they became blasé (they'd done it all before), couldn't be bothered and needed gentle persuasion!

Another plus was that the residents mixed and mingled around the tables. They could not lay claim to any of the patio chairs as they did to 'their' chairs in the lounge. The tables around which they gathered were small — they could lipread or hear each other's conversations easier. Some ladies and gentlemen had their lunches or teas out there — after all they had to dine indoors most of the year. Going to the dining table for meals served an equally important function. They had to move and exercise their limbs, sit next to or opposite different people from the ones to whom they sat near in the lounge.

One of the happiest sights for me was to walk outside on a sunny afternoon, residents resplendent in sun hats and glasses of various designs. Faces, arms (knees, if they should dare to pop out from under a skirt) all creamed against the ravages of the sun — and licking ice creams. More often than not with a smattering of visitors sitting amongst them boosting the conversations.

One gentleman sun-worshipped constantly — would not wear a hat, glasses or cream. And as for sitting under an umbrella — no way! Sometimes he could be enticed to sit under trees by sitting his best friend *in situ* first but then it involved carers silently and secretly changing the position of the parasols behind him because, most inconsiderately, the sun would keep moving around!

Carers had priority jobs to perform in the afternoons. Looking after the physical needs of the residents came top of the list but they also had to sort and put away the residents' laundry, washed and ironed the previous night. There was mid-afternoon tea to serve and afternoon teas to prepare — and a hundred and one other tasks that presented themselves. But if they had time it was good to see them sitting under the umbrellas with the residents, conversing or reading out snippets of interest from the papers, adjusting knitting or doing light mending.

Far from wasting time, this was an essential part of a carer's duties. This was the time when, fully relaxed, one could learn so much background and information about a person (not in a prying way) and although it may not seem of importance at the time, could be used at a later date to the benefit of that resident.

Ella owned an excellent walking frame. It had a seat, brakes and a carrier in which she transported books, glasses, gloves etc. Each morning when it wasn't raining or slippery under foot she walked around the garden, pushing her frame in front . . . until she found her sunbeam! This happened spring, summer, autumn and winter. At times the sunbeam was elusive and very slender and she needed to constantly move in order to keep in direct line and so be warmed. This was where the carrier came in useful. When she left the Home the layers of clothes she wore depended upon the strength of the sunbeam, and she would either dress up or strip down accordingly, taking when necessary gloves, scarves, hat or extra cardigans in the carrier under the seat.

When settled out would come a book and Ella would happily read while awaiting the morning cup of coffee. So regular was she and so tuned-in were the staff to taking the coffee to her that I have actually seen a carer speak to her indoors and STILL go outside to give her the coffee.

Reading was not the only interest she had in the garden. Often she would sit and watch the gardeners as they dug, weeded and pruned and together they would put the world to rights.

Another lady resident had an electric wheelchair. An excellent vehicle that gave her so much independence but, regrettably, she never really got to grips (literally) with the controls. Best not to stand behind her before she started to move — not if one wanted to keep skin on one's shins. Best not to stand directly in front of her either. Not if that was the occasion when she got it right. Not, if one did not wish to be ironed out over the path.

Grace suffered from the Seasonally Affected Disorder (SAD) syndrome and, although on medication to help alleviate the depression and lethargy she experienced through lack of sunlight, she still hated the wintertime and especially Christmas and New Year. During that season each day when given her early morning cup of tea she would squint through semi-closed eyes and moan, 'Oh bother! I'm still alive — I'd hoped I might have "gorn orf" in the night'. It was quite revealing however, that whenever she was ill or under par she fought harder than anyone else in the Home to get better and was the perfect patient.

And then came spring. And with it . . . buds. And then leaves on the trees. Right under her window. Grace loved this tree — a flowering purple-leafed plum. It was rich and vibrant and seemed to breathe life into her again. Often she was given the opportunity to move to a downstairs bedroom. 'No thank you dear, I cannot leave my tree.'

The lady in the room next to her equally loved those trees but for different reasons — she loved the pink flowers that would start to form in February. First there would be one minute head, the next day two. It was my job to count them with her when I delivered her breakfast. The next day, three and the day after, six. And then 12, 20, 30 — and we had to stop counting. Suddenly the tree exploded with thousands of pink flowers and I knew that soon Grace too would be happy.

The view from the next door window was again different. The incumbent of this room looked down into the centre of a lilac, its beautiful fragrance wafting up and through her open window. And so on, down the line. Down to the amelanchier. In late autumn and winter it looks nothing much — just a multi-stemmed jumble of a shrub. Then came spring and with it clusters of white flowers flooding every branch so that when the next lady looked down from her window it was as if she were floating on a cloud.

The residents downstairs had their perks too. My father had been a keen gardener and gave me cuttings of his honeysuckle for the garden. They were heavenly scented. Two of the downstairs bedrooms had them trained around the windows — one over the main entrance door and another over the trellis at the back of the herbaceous borders. And each year when they reached their full potential I blatantly indulged in my own personal reminiscence therapy.

Then came the budleas and with them a multitude of butterflies. Only three windows looked to the front and their occupants had the advantage of being able to see who was coming, going and what was going on. An extra perk was being able to look at the lovely stone-built house opposite complete with its own quota of trees, shrubs and greenery. So no one missed out!

Runner beans, gooseberries, blackcurrants, pears, plums and cooking apples. They too had their *raison d'etre*. Nothing escaped! More occupational therapy for the residents. Sitting either outside, in the kitchen or lounge, they sliced beans, topped and tailed gooseberries, peeled apples and strung blackcurrants. Exercising their fingers and mouths. Again, some of my residents were in different clusters and sitting in different formations. Some of the ladies (this seemed a ladies job) liked to do it for old times sake, some (probably) because they didn't like to say 'no', some said it was a way of saying 'thank you' — helping us as much as they could. One lady said, 'no way, I never topped and tailed gooseberries when I was at home and I certainly have no intention of doing it now', and thumped the table with her fist to emphasise the point.

We knew when we were beaten. She didn't top and tail gooseberries!

However, everything in our lovely garden was not always lovely. A few years previously I had bought (I cannot think why), a curry plant and had planted it against a wall of the Home and on hot, sultry nights we smelled like an Indian takeaway.

That was infinitely preferable to another shrub which I had planted very close to the patio doors of the lounge. It had small, pinky-red clusters of flowers and pretty greenery. Just right for depth and backing to some of the bunches of flowers visitors brought in for the residents. Its beauty belied its smell which was obnoxious and one of which a cat would have been proud! A great deal of our time was taken up making sure that the Home had no 'incontinent' odour to it at all in spite of the fact that many of the residents were either singly or doubly incontinent. We really did not need the plants ganging up on us.

So I really was mortified one morning upon going down to the kitchen for the night staffs' reports to hear that in between washing, ironing, commoding etc the residents they had crawled up and down over the lounge carpet desperately trying to sniff out the patch of offending odour! I never told them what it was — seemed sensible and prudent not to somehow. During the hot, sultry night they had opened the door and let in 'the smell'.

Some people never grow up — thank goodness! One gentleman went scrumping one day with my daughter at the bottom of the garden, filling his pockets and every other available space with apples. Not knowing this I looked at Harry when he passed me in the passage and thought that his hernia had become rampant. He had apples where it wasn't possible to have apples and probably not hernias either! What was even more worrying was that as he hovered by the kitchen door the next morning clad in only pyjamas, he was still producing apples from about his person! It was quite a relief to find Harry had simply reverted back to the old days when he had laid out apples in drawers — and there they were, nestling amongst his underwear!

'Can I help?' asked Bella. 'Nothing too strenuous'. 'I've got just the job' I replied. 'Dead head the daffodils'. A simple enough task one would think. I gave my helper a bucket into which she could put the dead heads. About half an hour later she announced she had finished. I was a little surprised because I could still see some. Maybe she was tired and leaving the rest for the next day. And then she handed me the bucket. Filled to the top with bright red and orange tulip heads. Still very much alive — or had been. The pergola which lead directly into the herbaceous garden had been under sown with them, bright and vibrant and now . . . only green, boring stalks.

In the insurance policy that I had at that time, specifically designed for residential care homes, there was a clause that covered me for murder and suicide. Until that moment I had only viewed it with slight amusement. Not any longer! Alternating with all those pious thoughts of — benefits of fresh air, stimulation of the appetite, exercise, interest, etc I had delicious ones imagining what form her murder would take — and WHEN!

We never told Bella what she had done. She would have been mortified and it would have been so unkind! But it caused a lot of laughter amongst the staff although not too much of it came from me!

BAD HAIR DAYS
is there a plumber in the house?

I don't think that the expression 'bad hair day' had been invented when we first opened the Home, but it was certainly a saying which was very descriptive of many of our days . . . and nights!

On one particular 'bad hair night' I was extremely lucky to be away. Not so fortunate for the nurse who was sleeping in our home to oversee events, in both my husband's and my absence.

As was a certain resident's wont, she got out of bed again very late in the night, switched on her television, used her commode and then washed her hands. Pity she forgot to turn off the taps and also a pity that the television was on so that she couldn't hear the running water. Water overflowed over the brim of her washbasin, over and through the carpet, eventually syphoning itself out through the rose of the central light into the bedroom below. There must have been a lot of water on the move that night (even more than usual) — just a trickle and the water-resistant carpets would have contained it. This in turn activated the fire alarms, which would not be silenced. It was rather reminiscent of *The Gas Man Cometh*.

The good news was that although the resident in the room underneath did not hear the bells, being extremely deaf, the regular drip, drip of water onto her face, her bed being directly underneath, would have eventually done so. The bad news was that her bedding became very damp before activating the bells and the arrival of carers.

More good news — as both my husband and I were away, there was a spare bed in our adjoining house, where the bedraggled lady could spend the rest of the night.

Yes, I felt very sorry for our nurse and damp resident and almost guilty — but not quite. You see, what can be described in one or two sentences actually took many hours to thoroughly sort out and settle everyone down again. It was work that continued into the next day.

The irony of the situation was that this particular resident seldom remembered to wash her hands after going to the toilet — she usually needed reminding!

While attending the management course prior to being registered by the county council to manage my own Home, our class would witness two of our peers rigidly glued to the telephone. Every coffee and lunch break! Their own Home was up and running, apart from the laundry system that should have been, but wasn't.

There were others who also were running their own Homes and were likewise a tremendous source of example and strength to me in those early days. I learned so much from them, although in my pre-Home state of ignorance I could kid myself that it wouldn't happen to me! I should have remembered those white, strained faces and knuckles!

If I could get past midday on Christmas Eve or Maundy Thursday without a major breakdown of any of the appliances, I was happy. If anything was going to go wrong it always seemed to do so when there was the maximum length of general holiday stretching ahead. I should have remembered my college days because, yes, it was always the washer or tumble dryer which did so. About seven or eight loads could pass through their drums each evening and night. They certainly earned their keep and rarely broke down but when they did it was horrendous. But we overcame! My staff and I had a good system going — if their machines broke down and if desperate they could use mine and if mine broke down, then they took our dirty washing home with them.

We had one other good system going — one of my members of staff's husband was a plumber and another was an electrician. It worked well because, if there was a problem, my ladies ensured that their husbands answered my SOS calls QUICKLY! Another lady was married to a fireman, although he of course could not answer my calls on his own!

A plea went out to my employees: was there anyone out there between marriages, about to be between marriages, would like to be between marriages, but hadn't told him yet? Before making the final selection for the new man in their lives we have vacancies for: carpenter, odd-job man, chimney sweep, decorator and blocked drains clearer. In the meantime my husband attended to the decorating, odd jobbing and sewage clearing. The only trouble was that he was away all day and if one needed the drains unblocking, then one needed him NOW! Then bliss. The part-time gardener said that he was good at that sort of thing — believe me, happiness was waking up in the morning knowing that such a person was close at hand. Why the need? Why indeed!

We verbally and emphatically instilled into our residents that they should never put continent pads down the 'loo'. This worked well with those who were mentally alert. What about the confused or forgetful? Mostly they were accompanied by a member of staff but a few fast walking forgetful persons could ruin the system. If they couldn't remember why they were wearing such articles or worse, were insulted as they saw it as a nappy, then they would remove it and the only place for it was obvious!

Our Home was created out of extending our own private home and once the building was completed we had our own flat on the first floor of the extension. Towards the end of the third year after the opening of the Home we again decided to enlarge it from 11 to 16 residents. This involved my husband and I moving out of our flat and having a house built adjoining the main building. This made room for the extra five rooms, a bathroom, separate toilet and a hairdressing area. Our flat had dissected the top floor. Initially this had not mattered as there were stairs both sides of the building but, as the residents became more frail, they could not walk up the stairs on the side of the building where there was no lift. It meant that half of the residents upstairs requiring the lift had to be wheeled through our lounge.

So, not only did we have a great demand for more bedrooms but we ourselves needed more privacy. And it made the first floor so much more efficient to run.

Privacy, demand and one or two other little things. There was that memorable time (for my husband) when he was awakened by a strange female, white from head to toe in flowing night dress, tweaking his big toe. I'm not sure who was the most astounded — him or the resident (who was a spinster) — to find a man in what she obviously thought was her bed!

Then there was the resident who, when being wheeled through our lounge, saw my coat slung over a chair. As he drew near to the crumpled heap he put out his hand and said, 'Good night, God bless, sleep well'. He thought it was me! How dare he! He was the resident with the very bad eyesight! He was the resident who lived very dangerously! As did the two carers who were escorting him and collapsed onto the floor in fits of laughter!

But I think the third example was the strongest reason for moving into a separate house.

I had placed a chair against our main door (we had to keep them unlocked to comply with fire regulations and freedom of access) as the occupant of the next door room tended to wander in the night. It was a carver chair, having arms and a detachable inner seat. Remind you of anything? Earlier I had gone into our home through another entrance and so far that day had not used that particular door. Later on during the morning I was walking along the passageway with one of the cleaners. The seat of the chair had been removed and was leaning against the wall.

'What's that doing there?' asked my cleaner, mystified.

'I cannot imagine', I replied, 'I cannot see any reason for dismantling it. Maybe someone tried to move it and found it too heavy.' Anyway, we put the chair together again, picked it up, turning full circle in its own space and moved it away. Imagination was no longer needed. We threw our shoes away!

The chair didn't need to be passed or even approached by staff or residents so no one on duty would have noticed it. And as for the running taps, well, it mattered not how well   we thought through any plan or system, it only needed just one resident, hard of hearing, slightly confused, poor eyesight, whatever . . . to cause havoc in the space of a few moments. It was not intentional, it could not be helped, but one relaxed and believed at one's peril! Never go out or to bed or even turn one's back and assume all would be the same the next minute because as every carer in the land knows . . . it won't be.

FIRE! FIRE!

Hot, sultry evenings and nights could be a major problem to the Home. Delicate sleep patterns of elderly people became fragmented, tossing around in bed, glad when morning came and with it, perhaps, a breath of fresh air. And still so tired. Fans were arranged around the lounge and kitchen in the daytime and in the bedrooms if needed at night. But it was always a relief when we got back to the good old cooler English days. Not more so than that the cooler air wiped out the thunder flies who would appear from nowhere in their thousands — a major nuisance.

For obvious reasons the fire and smoke detectors were of necessity incredibly sensitive — a thunder fly passing by or getting stuck on the sensor sent all the alarms off. It was too dangerous to assume it was merely a fly. Check lists for such occasions had to be adhered to, to the letter — day or night.

There were plenty of staff around during the day, evening and night. Two carers worked throughout the night, not only looking after the residents but also attending to the mountain of laundry which erupted each day. As well as the two carers there was always both my husband and myself (or at least one of us) and, if we were absent, our deputy slept in our house which was attached to the Home so she was on call. If it had ever been necessary, then there were two people to carry and one person to herd and lead the elderly people to safety. First having woken them up.

First having woken them up?! Fire bells are not designed to be slept through. Believe me! Each time they were activated I did a vertical take-off and had to scrape myself off the ceiling. The effect was instant and my staff and myself went into emergency mode immediately. How could anyone sleep through all that — even with only slight hearing? Oh yes, they could!

On one such occasion as usual in the middle of the night, I met a lady standing by the lift. Lifts cannot be used at such times in case the electricity goes off and there they would be, dangerously stranded. Fortunately she hadn't attempted to use it as she knew only to enter it when accompanied by a member of staff.

However, it did raise more questions. So the next morning I decided to conduct a survey with all the residents as to how they had initially responded to the bells the previous night. Well, most of them hadn't heard them because they had taken out their hearing aids!

One casually asked, 'whose room was the fire in?' What faith they had. Another said she had got out of bed and waited and another — the best yet — said, 'I put on my knickers and waited'.

Put her knickers on! This really impressed me because I had hurtled to the check point, hurtled into every room on the floor showing the red alert, bedrooms, airing cupboard etc either to check the alert 'eyes' or to check the emotional state of the resident, in about two seconds flat. Wearing only, at that point, my night-dress. Knickers didn't even enter my head. This resident's mother must have brought her up infinitely better than did mine. Being cleanly clad during the day in preparation for being run over by the proverbial bus was all I was prepared for. Being in receipt of a fireman's lift in the middle of the night had obviously not entered into my mother's imagination.

Fire prevention had to be taken very seriously. Wondering how anyone coped with evacuating (not always necessary of course, depending on the size and danger of the fire), even to another part of the Home, fuelled the imagination to nightmarish proportions. The movement of the frail, physically impaired status of my residents would have been so slow, so laboured — although they do say adrenaline works wonders in times of stress so maybe one or two might have managed to break into a trot. Then there would be the side effects of the smoke, stress-related heart attacks, strokes and so on. It was worth being careful.

It was also the law. Homes are regularly checked by the relevant fire authority. The Home made weekly checks on the bells and smoke alarms and were recorded. Annually the Home was officially inspected. Do all fire doors close correctly, exit doors not obstructed, fire extinguishers still in date, in correct position, not hidden from view, correct number and type? Spot checks were also carried out and were always more revealing than the pre-arranged ones. But it worked both ways. Any questions, queries, worries — it made more sense to ask the professionals than try to work it out oneself. Smoke detectors were regularly maintained, as were extinguishers which were re-filled or replaced as required. The local fire brigade visited soon after our opening and toured the Home, making itself *au fait* with the layout of the Home.

The Environmental Health Department checked out not only our food hygiene, temperatures of refrigerators, freezers, cleanliness in the kitchen, toilets etc and records of our own personal checks but also oversaw the safety aspect in the Home. The lift was maintained quarterly and inspected (for insurance purposes) half-yearly.

Each Home is allocated a registration officer — our Home being just one of many under her wing. During my owner/managerial life I had three different officers who carried out their duties to an excellent degree. When setting up a Home, rigid rules and regulations are set out (by the registration authority), annually inspected and again, spot checks are made. Prior to the prearranged inspection day copies of menus, staffing rotas, names of residents who had died during the past year and the reasons for their deaths, names and addresses of staff who had left and their reason for leaving — all this information and much more was sent to the inspection team. Information re: induction and training programmes for the staff — who attended and when and whatever evidence was required to confirm that the Home was being run correctly and to the benefit of the residents.

Accompanying the Registration Officer on the actual day was a lay inspector. They examined bedrooms and public rooms, checked fire and environmental health reports, talked to members of staff on duty and also to the residents, with whom they also ate their lunch. They looked deeply into care plans, medication reports and the safety of the medication cabinet and checked out 100 other items. Nothing went unnoticed — it was a thorough examination and a very long, tiring but essential day for both parties. And once again the system worked well — they oversaw that the running of the Home was correct but were there to advise should we need it.

Staff attended courses for both departments. Cooks, cleaners, carers all involved in fire awareness. Cooks, especially, were required to attend food hygiene and preparation courses. Carers too, if involved in the preparation of food, as indeed mine were for not only teas but also endless cups of tea, coffee, cold drinks for residents and visitors and night time milky drinks.

Mostly, these courses took place outside the Home but we particularly liked the Fire Authority to give demonstrations *in situ*. Seemed to make more sense. Videos were also shown and these really hit home. The reality of the utter horror of fire enveloping us, lingered on and hopefully never left us.

On one occasion the fire officer came to give us a talk quite soon after lunch. We were having it in the dining room and as he had arrived a little early — and certainly before I had rearranged the dining furniture — I showed him into the kitchen, gave him the kettle, milk and sugar and left him to his own devises, while I continued moving furniture.

The kitchen although without any actual partition was in two parts. The cooks' end with all the necessary cupboards, cookers, worktops etc and then, beyond that, it opened out into a second area with a large kitchen table, chairs, with patio doors leading out to a sun room. It was in this second area where any residents who were interested could help with the preparation of teas, making sandwiches, buttering scones — just like they used to.

The fire officer though was secreted in the cooks' area, tucked away in the corner. No need for lights, he could see quite adequately to make a cup of tea.

Shortly afterwards various members of staff came drifting in. One of the first to arrive had gone directly to the Home after buying herself several sets of underwear, having successfully just completed a slimming course. Always a good excuse for a binge and a present to oneself for being so dedicated! Thereupon she gave the rest of the staff a fairly intimate fashion show. At the same time the others were holding the garments up against themselves, talking about them at length, as they fluttered the flimsy garments against their bodies. No one had noticed the fireman.

Pity really!

When I arrived back from the dining room, I found him puce and cowering in the corner — afraid to come out. He had seen and heard too much to reveal his presence. Eventually we managed to cajole him out. Gradually he recovered his composure and even admitted to enjoying the experience! I understood that he liked the spotty ones best. And his lecture wasn't bad either. As for my new slim-line carer, well she didn't calm down until several hours later.

Then there was the time we went to the safari park. On this occasion everyone went, apart from a lady who was staying for respite who declined the invitation to go further afield. Two of my carers stayed with her — *just in case.*

During the afternoon the fire alarms were activated. No apparent reason but they could not get them to stop, maybe 'teething problems' as it was in the early days. Worried that there was an unseen problem festering away somewhere, the carers rang the fire station for advice. In the event a fire crew and engine arrived and the lady resident enthralled at all the goings on said it was the highlight of her stay! After all, a group of firemen in an engine are worth hundreds of lions in the bush!

Without doubt the most embarrassing encounter we had with the fire brigade occurred on . . . Christmas Day! It was, in fact, the only time we had anything like a real emergency. Unbeknown to me a visitor had put some wrapping paper on the fire and the next thing we knew we had our neighbours at the door alerting us to the smoke that was pouring out of the chimney. It was bad enough having a chimney fire and all that that represented but at 1.00 pm on Christmas Afternoon! The station was only two miles away but even so, the part-time firemen had to get from their homes. It was so impressive — they arrived within minutes. There were no problems, damage or heart attacks (well, only to me) and no mess to clear up.

But it was so EMBARRASSING!

Considering the number of times that the lift was used each day — 30 or 40 times — it behaved itself very well, only stopping between floors, due to a fault, three or four times in eight years.

Each new member of staff had to go through an induction programme. One of the items being (loosely translated) 'what happens if the lift breaks down with someone in it?' And no, the answer wasn't 'panic'. Even if one initially did! Each resident was always escorted so at least they weren't alone.

Early on in the history of the Home we had a respite lady called Beattie come in for convalescence. She was in her early 60s and normally very fit — able to walk unaided and look after herself but in for a one-off need of rest and assistance with her dressing. I'm not sure that she did get any rest though.

First of all she backed into a chair, chattering to someone and not looking where she was going she missed the chair and sat on the floor. Another day we were visiting a friend who was giving the residents a tea party in her own home and one of the legs fell off the chair on which Beattie was sitting. Majestically and slowly she slid to the floor. Luckily staff were sitting close and were able to support her as she lowered herself to the floor in fits of laughter. By far the worst incident though was when she was in the lift and it stopped between floors. The carer, Maggie, escorting her was quite extrovert and the two of them had great fun while Maggie performed a song and dance act to while away the time so that Beattie didn't panic. It obviously worked because as we learned later, Beattie actually suffered from claustrophobia. We were fortunate too in the circumstances that it only took two or three minutes to manually lower the lift. But Beattie never came back!

ANIMAL MAGIC

Animals had their part to play in the general wellbeing of the residents. Most residents had had a domestic pet of some sort in the past and welcomed staff bringing in their dogs, puppies and kittens — some so small that they were still lightweight enough to be borne on aged laps and stroked.

One of my carers had a mother who lived at an animal-lovers paradise. She had horses, dogs, goats, guinea pigs — to mention but a few! Living not too far away we were able to visit her from time to time with the more avid pet-lovers. One of her dogs was a massive German Shepherd called Sefton as soft as he was large and with whom one of my residents had a very special relationship. He knew her name and as soon as his mistress mentioned it he knew exactly where he was going. Upon arrival at the Home he went straight to her room, sat bolt upright in front of her — he on his haunches and she in her wheelchair, eyes on the same level just gazing and talking to each other. One could feel the rapport the moment one entered the room. Sefton boosted her morale far quicker than could mere humans!

The main attraction in the Home was without dispute the two cats — Fudge and Smudge. Smudge so called because he had a broad, black belt running naturally over his back but more commonly known as Big Ginge because that is what he was.

Fudge was the particular best friend of one lady, sitting on her lap by day and bed by night. One day she had a stroke which affected movement in her arm but that was the side that Fudge lay when in her bed. It was an automatic, natural reaction for her to try to stroke him and, as best she could, she continued to do so. He may well have been instrumental in aiding and speeding up her recovery in that area.

One morning sometime after her stroke I went into her and there she was, hanging on by her toe and finger nails to the side of the bed . . . laughing. 'Whatever are you doing?' I cried. 'Fudge pushed me out.' Throughout the night he had catnapped, awoken, yawned, stretched and each time he stretched, he edged her nearer to the abyss. And she didn't like to disturb him!

Her bones were brittle and very breakable. Whatever would the doctor or ambulance crew (if it had necessitated their help) have thought when questioning me if she had fallen to the ground and broken any bones? Would they have believed me when I answered that the cat pushed her out of bed? Unlikely! We didn't need cats as well as flowers and thunder flies ganging up against us!

Stroking cats is meant to be a stress-relieving exercise and I'm sure that usually it is, but not always. Believe me they can also cause stress. Stress to the staff and jealousy amongst the residents. Every so often they would change laps for no apparent reason and the situation would develop into a game of one-upmanship. It was usually the female laps that they sought out, presumably because their skirts provided a safer haven. A lady whose lap had been spurned after several weeks of pampering put on a brave face at the time but one just knew she would find some way of retaliation later on.

One lady in particular whose comfort had been rejected would stride across the lounge, pick up the offending cat off its preferred lap – hands squeezing its middle, its four legs hanging limply towards the floor and eyes bulging — as she retraced her steps. No arms free to facilitate an easy sit down herself, she would throw herself back into her chair, the momentum of which threw her legs upwards nearly touching the ceiling and upon reaching an acceptable position again would grind the cat into a sitting position on her lap as soon as possible. The cat would stretch and then majestically step from her seat, float across the floor, nose and tail stiffly upright and then equally slowly for maximum effect gyrate himself onto the lap of his choice. Then cat and chosen resident closed their eyes with satisfied smiles on their faces as they drifted off into a contented sleep.

I passed the rejected one a little later reading the newspaper with a lot of shaking and rustling of pages. Long distance glasses on her nose, newspaper upside down, spitting venom at all around her. And one just knew that although that battle was won, the war would rumble on and on . . .

One of the nicest characters in the canine world that visited us lived in the village. He was a fun dog, a scamp and a character. His master's mother resided in one of the upstairs bedrooms. It was one of his favourite walks because there at the end of it was a cupboard full of biscuits! He would hurtle through the door, attach his nose to the cupboard door and not move until he had had his fill. One day a brother of his master arrived to visit his mother.

'Where do I go?' he asked the family. 'Just take the dog' he was told. They pointed him in the right direction and he was off. Ears and tail streaming out behind him with brother hanging on to the lead, his hair and tie streaming out behind him too, body parallel to the path he covered the ground in record time. No time to knock or ring the bell, straight into the kitchen, two noses pressed up against the door. No one knew who he was and he didn't know us either. It didn't matter as we had a pretty good idea. 'I think you have my mother upstairs', he said sheepishly from his lowly position.

Big Ginge got through many lives. All the usual ones known to cats and two which were a little bit out of the ordinary. He lost his tail, traumatically, in a 'crossing the road' incident from which he completely recovered.

The other was more bizarre. He had been missing for about three weeks when one evening we received a telephone call from one of the staff. She had been driving through a village about six miles away and had seen a ginger cat lying hurt in the gutter. It had to be Big Ginge.

From the nearest house she had telephoned and arranged to meet my husband so he could go with the cat to the vet's. Carefully they took him from one car to another but alas, he was already dead. We were all terribly upset but grateful that he had been so lovingly looked after in his final hours.

Just in case

A fortnight later . . . he walked in through the back door! By chance at that moment I had been talking to his rescuer. Suddenly she disappeared from my line of vision — she'd collapsed in a heap on the ground. Understandably — she'd never seen anything rise from the dead before! Never mind, my carer had made some other poor cat's life more bearable at the end.

The garden sometimes attracted a highly coloured woodpecker. Birds would occasionally build nests around the patio and for two years we were visited daily by a pheasant. He nonchalantly pecked his way to us from two of our neighbours' gardens, into ours and performed for the residents strutting his stuff up and down in front of the window for all to see.

Twice a year there is that phenomenon called changing the clocks. 'I've altered all the clocks' sang out one of my night staff as I appeared in the kitchen one Sunday morning. A mammoth task as this involved not only changing the time in the communal areas but also the residents' wrist watches and clocks in their bedrooms. 'Oh! Thanks!' I said. 'Now perhaps you could change them all back again — it's not until next Saturday night.' She was not amused.

And so started a long leg-pulling pastime, involving members of staff — we all joined in ensuring that whatever members of staff were due in at 8.00 am (shift changeover time) on those two Sunday mornings, actually arrived at 8.00 am and not 7.00 am (unlikely) or tragically 9.00 am.

In the autumn of the pheasant's second year of visiting, the residents were seated in the lounge awaiting coffee at the new adapted time. When the pheasant appeared he was one hour early. No one had reminded him to change his clock! The residents loved it — as one they erupted with laughter. Who needed to spend large amounts on entertainment when we had it free in our own backyard?

BE PREPARED
emergencies & aids

Visits to the local hospital were pretty thick on the ground. Clinics to be attended — for eyes, hearing-aids, specialised shoes, dentistry. Minor operations to be performed, potential residents to be assessed, visits to residents who were residing in hospital for a few days for whatever was needed, hospital admittances and so on.

If it was for a routine check-up, the appointment turned into a wider outing. Coffee afterwards, followed by a detour home along unfamiliar or scenic routes. If the resident needed two to handle, then a carer would either offer or be coerced into accompanying us.

As already discussed, care plans are devised based on medical, social and other requirements. The resident, family and friends play a large part in this operation. For instance we knew that the lady, now wheelchair-bound, whom my carer and I were taking to hospital for an appointment used to be a brilliant ballroom dancer. A pity really that no one had mentioned also that she was an appalling back seat passenger because she was, at the time, sitting in the back seat directly behind me. She could not tell us that she suffered from travel sickness because her speech had been impaired due to a stroke. We got there all right. Feet measured and then back into the car. It was just about the time for the schools to come out and roads were particularly busy with nowhere to stop and no means of escape. It was that moment she chose to demonstrate the meaning of the saying ' to get it in the back of the neck'. I'm not sure which of the three of us felt the more ill by the time we got home, but from then on suitable receptacles were added to the collection of 'emergencies' that lived in the back of my car.

It was essential when going on outings, to take a good supply of 'emergencies'. *Just in case!* Therefore, the back of my car was alive with pants, knickers of every sort and shape imaginable, tights, stockings, hold-ups for fat legs, hold-ups for thin legs and hold-ups for every size in between, suspender belts, indigestion tablets, travel sickness pills, rugs for putting over legs etc, etc. And now sick-bags!

'Here you are, there's a present for you'. The daughter of one of my residents placed six duck eggs in my hands. Evidently another resident had accosted her on her last visit to the Home and, knowing that she kept ducks, not very subtly told her that they were her favourite eggs. I was just driving away so placed them amongst the rugs and cushions in the back so that they wouldn't break and promptly forgot all about them. Not only did I forget to take them out but forgot the entire incident. A few days later the daughter visited again and asked if the resident had enjoyed them. When no one could recall seeing them she asked me where they were. I couldn't remember. We searched high and low for days (in fact weeks) but they were nowhere to be seen. About six weeks later, when rearranging boxes in the car, I came across them, snuggled down amongst the cushions. What if they'd hatched out?

Not only did I need room in the back of the car for 'emergencies' and duck eggs but very often wheelchairs, walking-frames and sticks. In fact there were times when there wasn't a lot of room left for passengers.

Of course there are all sorts of aids to assist elderly and infirm people with easier access and transfer. One of these is a very simple but effective rotating circular cushion. Made in two main parts the base sits rigidly on the seat and the upper half, circular, moves in however large or small an arc one requires. With it placed on the front passenger seat all one had to do was to sit the resident sideways onto it. Then, with the carer's arms correctly positioned around the resident they could lift their legs and gently rotate them to an angle of 90 degrees when their legs should gently touch the floor and their body face the window.

It really is a good aid especially to someone living in their own home with, perhaps, just one carer to lever them in and out of cars. We regularly sent our residents out on visits to the relatives, clutching one of our circular seats. And at

Just in case

other times the seats joined my other 'emergencies' in the back of the car. Such a simple operation.

It was another outing. 'Wheee-ee', shouted Cissie, the child in her erupting out of her aged body. Bottom firmly placed on seat, hands pushing hard against the dashboard to make her swing faster. She covered an angle of 360 degrees before one could draw breath. Shrieks of laughter. Cissie laughed and laughed, her hair brushing the grit of the court-yard, her heels draped over the steering wheel and her body still rigidly set in the 'armchair' position. The carer was visibly shaken. Not so the resident — she hadn't had so much fun in years.

But at last we were away. The Great Outdoors beck-oned. I had, as always, my list of travellers just in case we left someone in a 'loo'! I was being silly. It couldn't possibly happen. They were always escorted, but once on that seat, left to their own devises for privacy — well, something unfore-seen could occur, deeming it necessary for the carer to move on temporarily to another job. It never happened, but *just in case*.

Most places that we visited had disabled toilets — big and wide with hand rails etc, but not all. This time we were at a friend's house for a cup of tea, having toileted our two car loads of residents prior to leaving the Home. It shouldn't matter that there was just an ordinary toilet in the house because, in addition, there was also an antiquated one in the garden for easier access but we really shouldn't need one. Wrong!

It was easy to get our rather large lady with the restricted movement onto the seat but getting her off was another matter. There were only narrow areas either side of her for the carers to get their bodies in the correct position and for easy leverage. And no hand rails for her to assist us with the exercise.

'Don't worry', cried one of the carers to the others, leaping to the rescue. 'You stand either side in front of her and pull and I'll stand behind her and push'. Standing behind her on the back of the toilet and bin, legs astride, meant having her head stuffed up the old-fashioned cistern. Brilliant, apart from one thing, the resident started to laugh. She laughed until she was a wobbling mass of jelly. The carer laughed too. In fact she laughed and laughed . . . and laughed until suddenly she discovered the true meaning of stress incontinency. The resident was all right. She was sitting in the appropriate place! But in future we added the 'take anywhere' extra-height toilet seat to our back of car 'emergencies'.

Yes, seats featured largely in our everyday lives — and not only toilet seats of the extended-height variety. Although they, along with ordinary seats and bath-hoist seats, were among the most important areas which had to be kept scrupulously clean and hygienic for obvious reasons — as did the bottoms of all the baths.

What about chair seats? Taken so much for granted. They had to be of varying heights to accommodate varying lengths of leg and comfort and support for backs.

Often residents brought in their own favourite chair from their own home — one of the strongest and most comforting links with their past. Often these chairs could be instructed to take up various positions to suit the individual by just the touch of a button or movement of a lever! These chairs were kept in their rooms and were their own private property — apart from one lady who preferred hers to be in the general lounge and, quite rightly, none of the other residents sat in it.

I really wish that I hadn't either! I really wish that I hadn't sat in it to be adjacent to a resident to whom I wished to talk. I really wish that I hadn't absent-mindedly dropped my fingers down the side of the cushions, come in contact with the lever and with a flourish brought it upright. Before I knew it I had been ejected from the chair in one enormously high arc only making contact with the carpet again, several feet away with my body still in the 'armchair' position. I was then bounced upwards and forwards again — my flight only being abruptly halted by contact with the patio window and a slow-motion fall to the ground. I was reminded of the Tom and Jerry cartoons of my youth. The major difference being that Tom, after being hijacked or booby-trapped by Jerry and coming up against a solid object, regained his senses and normal feline shape within seconds. With me it took several days. But NO ONE blinked an eyelid or expressed surprise! For goodness sake, I didn't normally move around in such an exaggerated manner . . . did I?!

Cissie was going out for lunch and an early tea so she would be back in time to freshen up before an evening entertainment in the lounge. Her son took the rotating circular cushion with him. 'Whatever you do, do NOT let your mother loose in charge of the rotating circular cushion', we instructed him. He looked at us in utter disbelief. Whatever were we talking about? We described in detail the hazards of letting elderly ladies loose with that sort of cushion.

Mother behaved with great decorum, whenever in contact with it. Son was most impressed with the accessory. 'I've got another in my room', his mother informed him upon their return. 'It's for standing on. It helps me to turn easily when moving from my wheelchair or chair to bed. Do you want to see? I'll show you how it works, while you're here.' Oh! The innocence of it all.

Both feet firmly placed on the cushion, carer's hands guiding and supporting in correct position. Look of boredom on son's face. 'Whee-ee', she cried as she pushed with all her might against the back of the chair. The speed with which she spun twirled her round and round. More and more she pushed and if the carer hadn't grabbed her by her coat-tail she'd have been out of the door like a white tornado.

'Now do you believe us?' we asked him. Yes, he believed. 'Would you like to stay on for the entertainment?' 'No, no I think I'll just go home', he replied faultingly. Enough was enough.

There was the occasion when a helicopter equipped with a winch would have been an invaluable asset. The time in question was while visiting the home of one of my carers. There in all its pristine glory stood my carer's husband's motorbike.

The group of residents included Harry, the apple-scrumper. 'Can I sit on it for a moment?' he pleaded. It was large and powerful — just the type he used to ride in his youth.

It seemed a reasonable enough request. Astride the machine he lovingly ran his fingers over the bodywork, fingered the brakes, accelerator — memories and excitement of days past flooded over him. It brought tears to the eyes! No crash helmets or black leathers in those days — wind streaming through his hair as he did the ancient equivalent of a 'ton-up'.

Just in case

Then it was time to get him off. Unfortunately . . . although Harry could swing his leg forward to mount the bike he was no longer capable of swinging it backward to dismount. Neither could he swing it forward and higher to clear the handlebars. Panic! Oh for the helicopter and winch!

Harry was perfectly happy and safe and didn't care if he had to sit on it all day. It took a lot of discussion, concern and various plans of action laced together with fits of helpless laughter and we did eventually prise him off the seat. But he was set in the 'vroom, vroom' position for days.

Goodbye, have a lovely time and don't you dare keep ringing in. We'll ring you if needed'. My staff were seeing me off the premises! Once a month I had a long weekend away and, if not with my husband, then I would stay with family or friends. Just to switch off so that I could go back home refreshed.

The nurse who oversaw the medicine and made the medical decisions in my absence was also on call while I was away. *Just in case!* The carers, cleaners and cooks were more than capable of running the rest of the Home for a day or two. They knew the needs and wants and care plans intimately. I was so lucky in that I could go away completely confident that the residents would be looked after as well as if I were overseeing duties, or not. Most of my staff had had years of experience and had been with me from the start and knew the Home inside out.

Nevertheless I had, as usual, left them with huge lists and several emergency contingency plans. Totally unnecessary but at times I became rather neurotic (emergency plans A-F on this occasion)! Got down the road and thought of plan G. Better not go back. Didn't want to be lynched.

Every time I went away I meant to change the cassettes in my car but every time I forgot. So the winding-down stage followed a regular melodic routine. It started well with Shirley Bassey. I belted out Shirley Bassey, windows wide open — who cared, no one could hear? Sometimes I needed to repeat the complete cassette again if especially stressed out. Then on to Lesley Garrett. I didn't attempt to accompany her — there were limits! Next was easier and calmer — a sing along with excerpts from Gilbert and Sullivan and so on to Perry Como (yes, really). He was so soothing. The magic was working well. Nearly to my destination and John Betjeman was beckoning. John Betjeman reading Betjeman. Bliss!

Bassey, Garrett, Gilbert and Sullivan, Como and Betjeman could all be relied on to de-stress me. Well actually Bassey, Garrett, Gilbert and Sullivan, Como and Betjeman and three bars of Kit-Kat, one Mars, a Flake and a packet of Jelly Babies (not so messy). Together they had done the trick and two hours later I was happily parked outside my friend's home.

That day we were in a hurry. Dressed in our best outfits we were dining in a smart hotel, ten or so miles away.

Driving and eating chocolate isn't always easy but I had mastered a technique whereby I could deflect the flaking pieces away from my lap and onto the passenger seat. Usually I placed paper over it to catch any crumbs but due to the speed with which I left the Home I hadn't bothered.

It was a scorching hot day. As I opened the door of my car for my friend, both our eyes were riveted on the brown, bubbling witch's brew of a mess. My friend looked aghast. 'I couldn't possibly sit on that', she said. Certainly not and if we washed the seat it wouldn't dry quickly enough and probably leave a nasty stain. 'I know', I said, leaping out. 'I've got just the thing'. Out to the back and in with the largest incontinent pad I could find. 'There you are, sit on that.' At that she looked, if possible, even more aghast. Horrified. 'No', she said, 'I couldn't possibly sit on that.' 'Yes you can, it's

Just in case

quite comfortable, I understand.' 'No, I mean . . . well really
. . . well . . . what if someone saw me?' 'I'll drop you off in a
dark alleyway and then you'll be okay.' By the time we were
at the bottom of the avenue she could see the funny side of it
and snuggled down to enjoy the drive.

From time to time I had wondered if I should wear one
of those baby bibs with turn-up rims to catch the flakes of
chocolate but decided against the idea. After all, what would
happen if I were involved in an accident or stopped in a police
road check? One look at my bib and all the odd articles and
aids and dress in the back of the car and I should certainly
have been taken in for 'further questioning'. But there were
times when the emergency supplies came in useful!

EMBARRASSING

MOMENTS

we've had a few

Now I'm not a superstitious sort of person. I don't mind going out of the front door when I entered by the back. I will pass anyone (within reason) on the stairs and crossed knives mean nothing. However, there are two superstitions about which I am careful. I do not willingly walk under ladders in case the tin of paint, hooked above me, empties itself over my head. The other is — if two 'somethings' untoward or nasty occur then I do like to get the third out of the way as quickly as possible so that I can get on with the rest of my life with an easy mind.

Three such 'somethings' occurred to me over a succession of weeks.

Each week I would roar into the nearest town, do the banking and other odd jobs, call into every new grandmother's favourite toy shop for a little light relief (as all grandmothers do) and then up the main street to that store which has an outlet in the centre of most towns. It was there that I bought gooey desserts and speciality dishes for residents' birthdays and other special occasions.

I may have given the impression that I cannot operate without a bar of chocolate in my hand. Not so. I can mind over matter it with the best of the chocoholics when in the mood for it.

We all know that every checkout in the land is a mine-field of chocolate bars. But not on this occasion. Oh no! This time I would overcome. My eyes wandered idly over the layers of coffee, almond, milk and caramel, and true to form my hand hovered over the racks while the mind battled with the tortured decision. I suddenly 'came to', realised what I was about to do and dropped my arm to my side. Unfortu-nately the lady on the till was experiencing difficulties with the current payer which gave me time to lapse into another trance. Up went the arm again . . . Turkish delight, or maybe jellybeans (so much cleaner to eat when driving down the spiral of the car park exit road). The queue started moving and I surfaced and forced my hand away. To a crescendo of applause! The five or six fellow queuers had watched with amusement and baited breath, my battle from within. So impressed were they with my temporary burst of willpower! We all laughed and an instant rapport was established — all of us failed weight watchers. Presumably!

The next week found me in the queue again. This time the embarrassment was infinitely worse.

When I first opened the Home a cabinet containing a stack of lockup compartments had been installed for the staffs' personal belongings. In the event this was never used as such as there was no need, we happily found, to lock anything up. We all kept our bags on the kitchen table. All black and of the 'shoulder bag' type. In fact more or less identical.

One carer on one occasion had driven home — six or seven miles away — opened her bag for the house keys and found it was the wrong bag. I shouldn't have teased her but it seemed funny at the time even if she didn't quite share the joke.

So there I was in that queue again, getting my comeuppance and with a nice tailback of voyeurs, witnessing all. I put my hand into my bag to pay the bill. No familiar purse, no familiar rectangle of plastic. In fact, nothing familiar at all. Puce with embarrassment I stuttered out that I had got someone else's bag. I left the trolley and ran. What a waste of a journey!

'Please let the third "something" come quickly and be fairly painless', I said to myself over and over again. The next week at the same checkout, in the same store, it did. But there was nothing painless about it.

From time to time I would have to extract a sample of urine from a resident to take to the surgery for analysis. It was really quite an easy matter — once obtained, slip the see-through phial into a plastic bag, place in my handbag and drop off at the surgery immediately. For some reason (the exact details of which have been lost in the mists of time), the sample was not needed after all. At that point I switched off about it and forgot it to such an extent that it remained in my bag for two or three days. Not, of course, to be recommended!

One week later and I was back in the queue. My purse had opened in the previous shop, dropping all the loose change into the bottom of my handbag. It didn't matter — I could sort it out later.

The lady at the till recited the amount owing. I handed over the paper money and then put my hand to the bottom of the bag to scoop out a handful of change. Also a phial of very yellow urine. It popped out of the bag and rolled slowly and majestically along the platform until it came to a stop, nestling amongst the awaiting empty plastic bags.

This time no one laughed and they certainly did not clap! The silence was thick with shock, horror and nausea. I felt all eyes transfixed on the offending object. I looked to neither left, right nor upwards — just picked up the phial and ran, head bent, out of the store. And I hadn't bought even a jelly-bean on which to drive home!

My embarrassing moments were not restricted to shopping in the high street. They could happen anywhere.

I used to suppose the reason that owners or managers persuaded relatives of residents to take them for their hospital appointments was perhaps due to lack of staff, time, etc. Not so. After quite a short period of such journeys I realised it was probably a case of how much embarrassment one could cope with in a short while.

On one occasion Marjorie and I went to the reception area in the hospital to book in. Marjorie was in her wheelchair for quickness of movement but, as we stopped, she rose from the seat to register her name. Instead of words coming out, an enormous gust of wind issued forth and through the small aperture of the window, spread-eagling the receptionist against the opposite wall. On the Beaufort Scale it probably registered hurricane velocity. I was just grateful that it issued forth from one of her front-facing orifices.

Because I was standing behind her!

It was another hospital and another resident. It was mid-winter. My gentleman was there for a consultation concerning a small melanoma on his face. He could remember where he lived but he could not remember why he was there. He thought he was there about his eyes and told them he wasn't worried about the lump on his face as he assumed it was frostbite and not to worry because it was always there and we would scrape it off again when we got home!

It sounded as if he lived in arctic conditions. As any one knows who has ever set foot in a Care or Nursing Home, we operate in tropical temperatures. The staff and I lived in summer dresses when at work whatever the season. But some-how there never seemed much point denying all the outrageous things which were said — it just made it seem as if it were true and the more I denied it, the deeper I could feel myself digging that hole!

OUTINGS

and counting them all back

I'm not sure when I first became an avid head-counter — but it was probably in the first couple or so years of this work. An unnecessary occupation one might think. After all, the residents couldn't exactly run away and hide. No, but there were other reasons . . .

On one occasion and one only, everyone was fit and well enough to go out. The WHOLE Home was to be away for the day — whooping it up!

We arranged in which cars our residents were to ride — and rearranged the pattern for roughly 16 different reasons. Only 16? By the time they were all safely and comfortably in their seats it seemed more like 116. About to roar off into the great unknown one of the helpers casually asked if a certain lady had changed her mind. She wasn't on board.

Good gracious! Yes, she certainly was going with us and there she was, sitting in her wheelchair in her room, hat and coat in position and handbag firmly clutched between her gnarled fingers. Totally unaware of the trauma to which we almost subjected her.

The bubbles of fear and horror didn't leave any of us all day and continued, in my case, for evermore. What if we had gone off, everyone thinking she was in someone else's car? What if she had remained there, virtually all day and totally alone? It didn't bear thinking about. I should, deservedly, have been tried for cruelty and shut down. If one resident only had not wished to accompany us then it would have entailed staff remaining behind to look after him or her and that particular problem would not have arisen. Would the good news have been that at least she couldn't walk unaided and therefore would have remained all day in one place — or was that the bad news? Thank goodness it didn't happen. And so the necessity of head-counting was born.

'Going out for the day' conjures up such happy thoughts for the uninitiated. The words have such a pleasant, laid-back, easy-going ring to them. And, yes, they were wonderful times. I think the main pleasure for the staff though, was seeing their residents so happy and 'opening up'.

Going out for the day, in reality, entailed a lot of fore-thought, planning and contingency plans . . . going on *ad infinitum*. The winkling of old and stiff limbs in and out of wheelchairs, cars, seats. The manoeuvring of wheelchairs through doorways, around tight corners, along narrow path-ways or even roads whose cambre was not true and at times could throw a wheelchair into the path of oncoming traffic, meant one had to be fully alert at all times. It meant the carers' arms, backs and legs were being put to maximum use and by the end of the outing . . . exhaustion!

And when we got home, everyone needed the toilet immediately. They needed a cup of tea immediately and after that, they all needed to go to bed at precisely the same time as each other — and immediately! But it was still worth it.

The more residents going out the more helpers were needed to escort, always bearing in mind that some carers would need to remain at the Home to assist and entertain those left behind.

Sometimes we hired a minibus, backed-up by individual cars and other times, depending upon the availability of drivers, we used just private cars. It was swings and roundabouts — a resident could see more from a higher platform but the cars offered more comfort.

Lists? I always made them but what was the use? I don't think we ever ended up adhering to them but it was a necessary occupation.

If one is fit and able swinging into a car presents few problems. Octo- and nonagenarians racked with arthritis, pains, aches, and beset with the limitations of strokes, do not easily swing anywhere.

A resident with a set, rigid leg cannot, because of lack of leg room, usually sit anywhere but in the front seat. Very large, heavy and dependent ladies and gentlemen do not easily manoeuvre into a back seat — in fact, they cannot. And so on. Often we needed more cars to take our residents out than we would have needed for physically able-bodied people because so many needed front seats.

Then there were the traumas of the back seat. One lady would refuse to share it with ANY gentleman. She would never say why (and we really would have LOVED to have known) — just purse her lips, fold her arms and grimace! In a large car with three ample seats in the back, sitting an able-bodied person in the middle should not have presented any difficulties. The only one who gladly took up this position was so tall that she completely obscured my view through the back window and another one, so much shorter, would not allow any part of any other person to touch her — regardless of the sex. So she couldn't sit there either. She insisted on there being two feet (measurement-wise) between her and the next person.

There were also the 'inseparables' until that was, five minutes before the outing when they suddenly became 'untouchables', not only refusing to sit beside each other but refusing to travel in the same car. And why did the ablest and most supple, sit-anywhere-person always seem to suffer from travel sickness and therefore require the coveted front seat? Over the years we had several of those. But it didn't dampen the outings.

One of the highlights of the year was attending the Lions spring party. Old-age pensioners from a wide radius descended on the town one Saturday afternoon in May. Coaches, cars, minibuses overflowing with elderly people and some went on foot — all converging on the local high-school.

The Lions, their ladies, entertainers etc worked hard to make it a brilliant afternoon out for everyone. The behind the scenes work paid off and the events of the afternoon flowed effortlessly. It wasn't just the lovely food and entertainment which made the day so special — another aspect emerged to present a 'plus'. In this case the 'plus' for my residents was the renewal and re-acquaintance of old friends. Friends who could no longer drive themselves or were wheelchair bound with no easy way of physically keeping up friendships. On this day however, they were all there together. Meeting again, exchanging news, catching up on gossip — just like old times!

Lovely tea, good general entertainment and then the comic. They loved him — mainly, I suspected, because he was so rude. They giggled over his jokes for weeks, recounting them time and time again to the staff and visitors. It always amazed me that they could hear so well, remember so well! Totally out of their norm! And if they could remember the jokes (and more importantly, the punch-lines), why couldn't they remember they had just told the joke five minutes earlier — and five minutes before that too?

Although I helped with the transport, I often did not stay, but two members of staff always accompanied the residents to help them to and from the toilet (and often waifs and strays too who were there on their own), serve their teas and see that they had all they wanted. It gave me a chance to catch up on outstanding issues or even do nothing.

As with most intervals, the audience left the auditorium and wandered around. Most of the audience were quite mobile. As with most buffet teas, it was difficult to balance cups, plates, serviettes and still have fingers left with which to manipulate the food. Little ladies with short legs tend to have little short laps, most of which sloped away from them so when it came to a balancing act — they couldn't and it seemed like a good idea to place one's cup and plate on the vacated seat in front. It would have been an even better idea if my resident had rescued her cupcake from the seat before the gentleman sat down again.

There were five ladies in that row. Behind him they laughed so much they nearly fell off their seats. They laughed for weeks. 'Did you tell him?' I asked. 'No!'. Stupid question. 'And when', they continued, 'he walked away, he was still wearing the paper case.' 'Yes,' said another, 'he was wearing his best suit too. Oh yes, that particular outing was very popular.

Not only did my residents meet old friends again when out but they also met new friends. Friends from the village 'Over Sixty Club' whom they had not known before. This was one of the major benefits — the inhabitants of the Home meeting others, being part of a greater community. It is all too easy for a Home, regardless of its situation, to become isolated and insulated from the rest of the world. It was great for my residents, when out, to be hailed and greeted — it raised their self-esteem. They were still 'alive', still interesting and other people wanted to know them and talk to them. Wonderful!

The Club was held once a month in a hall on the outskirts of the village. Those ladies and gentlemen well enough and interested were taken by car. The entertainment and the drive were not too long so they did not become too tired. Slides, talks, singers, tea and biscuits. These were the bases onto which a friendly rapport could be built. It was through this Club that they were invited to a farm on the edge of the village. Another outing for which to pile on the make-up, nail varnish and a chance to eat all those fattening cakes, which most knew they shouldn't. Even better, if the weather was lovely, they could all sit outside under the trees and indulge in the tea served up by members of the local WI. More people to talk to when out and more people to be visited by — the club organiser and her helpers to mention but a few. Spin-offs occurred, the chairman helped with transport. He was excellent – he knew whom he could sit with whom and who had the front seat of the car! He was deeply interested in wild flowers, wild life in general, had marvellous slides of the same and was pleased to show them in the lounge when requested.

En route to the Club, one gentleman could point out the three (or was it four?) houses he had lived in and then he could point them out again on the way back. This was when the system worked well — someone born in the village and a person who had represented his village on many committees on so many occasions could also live his last days, and hopefully die, in the village. He usually deserted his fellow residents when there. After all he could see them any day! No, he was back with his old mates, making the most of his time out. He could tease the Home's ladies any time — now it was some-one else's turn! The local ex-postmistress and later paper-lady, born in the village, also attended. It was so nice for the members to see her again after she had served them so well for so many years.

Each year we took our residents into the village to watch the spring bank holiday jollifications which took place in The Square. The first year we sat in a row on our own. No one knew us very well. Not for long. Thereafter the villagers made sure we were part of them — crossing the road to talk and mingle. It was in The Square that the decorated tractors, wagons, lorries, prams and bicycles assembled. And the majorettes, visiting bands, fancy dress contestants and Morris dancers got themselves sorted out. It was there they danced or played the first lines, in front of us, before progressing around the village.

We took them by car or pushed them in wheelchairs — carers, cooks and cleaners all helping with the transport and transfers. The local pub kindly supplied chairs for them, where once again, they sipped their sherrys, drank their beers and crunched their crisps. Everyone was happy. It was wonderful entertainment — the fun, the bustle and all those people to watch!

And every year Nature got in the way. The first year we sat our entourage outside the pub in the shade. It was a hot day so it seemed sensible. We had just got them in place when the wind got up, sped along the road, twirled and pirouetted around The Square, before whipping itself up into a frenzy and blowing straight up the residents' legs. A quick move was necessary although, because of the nature of the Home, no move was ever quick.

We learnt from our mistakes. Oh yes, frequently. All the time. The next year we sat on the opposite side of the road but because the sun was shining strongly we placed our chairs and wheelchairs under an overhanging tree. An overhanging lilac tree actually, filled to the gunnels and overflowing with bees who gleefully watched the whole performance of carefully placing residents under them, watched the carers retreat and then attacked in their thousands. Once again we moved.

But we would get it right. The next year because it was just pleasantly warm they sat in the sun, out of the wind and several yards from the lilac tree. No problem. First orders were placed, pleasantries exchanged between villagers and residents. The village Square was packed as were all the exit roads.

The sun burst through the clouds and instantly the temperature shot up and out of the top of the barometer and the residents visibly wilted. I'd forgotten the sun hats, glasses and cream! How could I have been so careless? I would have to go home and collect them. It was difficult enough to drive into an area where all the roads were closed — getting out was an even greater problem. It took time but I got there and back before anyone actually passed out. By which time the procession had moved on and I'd missed all the performances.

Yes, happy memories, it was good being part of that particular community.

The residents were sitting innocently in the two front rows at the pantomime. It was another local outing — another time to meet friends from one's past.

'Do you remember me?' one of the residents asked another who had seemingly been abandoned in her wheelchair next to her. 'No.' 'Well, you used to live near me. Do you still live there now?' 'I don't know.' 'Who are you with?' 'I don't know.' My resident saw panic welling up in her old neighbour's eyes. 'Never mind,' she said 'we'll look after you, you can come home with us.'

And thus it was we nearly received another resident. We were registered for 16, an extra would have had the same implications as accommodating illegal immigrants. Fortunately another resident alerted a carer before the gentleman who was assisting with transport (and did not know my residents) helped her aboard.

Head-counting? Essential. Upon arrival home, I invited the driver in for a cup of tea. 'No thanks,' he said wearily, 'I've got to get home.' Loosely translated, I think that read 'No thanks, I've got to go home and lie down in a darkened room for a while.' After an outing we all knew that feeling!

TEAM WORK
many helping hands

The local community supported us well. Visitors popped in unannounced, ladies took their exercise walking to the Home and back from the village, visiting not only old but new friends too. Yet another came by bus from the nearest town, to see old neighbours and members of the church they had all attended at one time.

Another filled our deep freeze with her excess of blackberries, runner beans and cooking apples. Then there was the very dear friend who had supported, and at times led, me through difficult times when setting-up the Home. Always at the end of the telephone to encourage and strengthen when the going got heavy and visiting and supporting all of her friends who became residents in later years. And as if that were not enough, overseeing the Home from time to time so that we could escape for a few days. There were also the two nurses who consecutively took over the Home when I was away, each doing an excellent job, keeping everything under control and allowing me time to relax. And then there was the gardener and the wages clerk.

The newspaper agent who, every time we changed our respite visitor, suffered a change of our delivery order. The village shop providing all our fresh meat, bread, fruit and vegetables and delivered to and supported the Home when I was away.

Overheard in that village shop and recounted to me at a later date: 'Who is that woman? She comes in here every day, staggers out with all that shopping and never pays for a thing!' 'Oh,' came the reply, 'she runs that place in the village.' Making it sound like a place of ill-repute. In answer to the first remark, there were twelve horrendous days of reckoning each year and to the second implication — no, it most certainly was not!

Ministers from all the denominations supported us. Not only did the residents receive Holy Communion every fortnight from our local vicar but the Roman Catholic Father in the neighbouring town administered also to his flock every Friday morning.

The inter-denominational Bible Reading Fellowship, led by the Congregational Minister, brought us extra services of readings and hymns before Easter and Christmas — plus little 'goodies' for the residents. The churches brought us Nativity plays and jazz bands, to mention but a few.

Individual ladies and gentlemen entertained us with monologues, slides and talks, duos sang, as did quartets, and sextets and groups sang, acted and larked about, bringing laughter, smiles and participation to all present. Brownies, Cubs and Rainbows (when Rainbows grew up they turned into Brownies) and other groups of youngsters all entertained over the years. Some ladies and gentlemen still managed to nod off, go to the toilet, lose their teeth, hearing-aids and glasses before, during and immediately afterwards — this wasn't the sole prerogative of the Holy Communion service.

The families of the staff got involved too. Sometimes with transport, talks, mothers brought in pets, granddaughters and others danced and sang and some played musical instruments.

One carer's husband and children were directed (instructed, bribed?) to keep one lady resident company for the Christmas tea party. She would have been the only resident without any of her family and without guests and would have hated it. What a kind family — they gave her so much pleasure that afternoon. She felt as important as everyone else in the room.

The most valued support came from the medical community. We received tremendous help from the doctors, district nurses, community psychiatric nurses and pharmacist. Constantly. Always there when needed. Life would have been so much more difficult (going on intolerable) without it. On many occasions, while standing in a queue for a coffee, while attending a course or listening to a lecture in some far-off town or county, I would listen to conversations going on around me regarding the back-up some received or didn't and wondered if we were on a different planet.

It didn't stop there. The backup from the dentists, chiropodists, optician, physiotherapist, social workers and registration officer — all doing domicillary calls, undertakers (definitely domicillary calls) and florists, was so strong too. One never had to wonder if the support and backup would be there when needed as it always was.

The Lions sent us Father Christmas and his elfin helpers with their Christmas carols the week before Christmas. It was fun. Again, some of the visitors knew our residents. I am not so sure that our residents knew them, in their festive outfits. It didn't matter, it was another excuse for wine, sherry, mince pies or whatever the residents and visitors felt like.

Often I would be walking along the road in a nearby town and a gentleman would smile and say 'hello'. Calling me by name so he obviously knew me and I presumably should have known him. On these occasions I often thought, 'if only he were wearing a fireman's helmet or a pixie hat wound around with white cotton wool I should know exactly who he was.' I suppose I should have said, 'sorry, I don't recognise you with your clothes on', but it might not have gone down too well!

'Come down to the lounge tonight', I would entreat a certain lady. 'We have a wonderful choir coming in.' 'No dear, I don't think I'll bother. I really only like the Bach choir or Philharmonic Orchestra or people like that'! There was really no answer to that refusal. But where did she think I would put so many people and instruments? However, everyone else, staff included, loved the evenings when choirs serenaded us.

The WI choir came too — popular and entertaining. Many of them old friends of the residents, many of them helped us in other guises during the year — helping with the Wednesday Club, serving teas in gardens, part of the religious services or even just visiting. Whatever 'hat' they were wearing they were welcome.

Twice a year a choir drawn from the surrounding district came to entertain us. It was so nice. We could look and see the florist, the librarian who helped to order cassettes for our visually impaired resident, the bank clerk, cub leader and many, many more — all conducted by the music teacher from the local school. She was hypnotic. The standard of singing was very high and they gave us a very special evening.

Sometimes, if in the summer, it was warm enough to have the patio doors open, we could spill onto the lawn — and it was magical.

One resident was a special favourite with this choir. He knew every music-hall song ever written and somehow, at some stage, he would subtly change the format of the evening and end up teaching them songs! No one minded. In fact I think the choir enjoyed it. He was a brilliant character.

One choir, now sadly disbanded, always entertained in full evening dress. Wonderful voices, monologues, dressing-up — it all made the residents feel extra special. They loved it — joining in when appropriate. They were with us during the week of celebrations to commemorate VE Day. The only way to finish that particular concert was with *Land of Hope and Glory*. They even supplied their own Union Flags to wave.

The next day spurred on from the interest evoked from the previous evening, the afternoon carers arranged all the dining tables in a row, decorated them with bunting and had an impromptu indoor 'street party'. The residents loved it and were uplifted by it. And for some totally unrelated reason the two carers broke into a sand dance . . . Who cared, the whole thing was hilarious?!

No, it wasn't fun and laughter all the time, but we tried . . . Many of the days the staff were run off their feet. Hardly a second to spare, so many problems, illnesses, worries, jealousies between residents etc — all to be sorted out. All on top of the common tasks of the every day basic caring duties, most of which were taxing and wearying. Exhausted at the end of their shifts and sometimes (but not too often) having to endure rudeness and verbal abuse from the person they were attending to. But then, suddenly, all problems seemed to peel away and that wonderful commodity called spare time came into its own.

'Doesn't seem natural', the staff would say, 'doesn't seem right'. 'Don't knock it', would be my reply, 'make the most of it, it could all go away any minute.' And make the most of it they certainly did.

Those were good days. Days when the staff had time to sit in either rooms or lounge and talk and play games with the residents. I think the afternoons that the residents liked the most (well they didn't have to exert themselves) were on miserable days, cold and wet outside, sitting around the fire and just talking. Carers read extracts from the day's newspapers, local information and gossip was bandied about.

They played Trivial Pursuit. Not in the way the inventors had intended. No, that would have been far too easy!

Our way was: carer stood in the middle of the floor, selected a card and asked the question. Better than going into a group of people and asking, 'what should we talk about?' because no one would have answered. The different subject matters drew everyone into the conversation. The fact that no one or very few, knew the answers, was of little importance. One thing led to another and there they were, all discussing topics, amicably arguing and giving us insights into their past lives and backgrounds.

They played soft ball and croquet in the lounge — but not very successfully. Nowhere near as popular as Trivial Pursuit. Then there was 'Group Grope'. This involved filling a stocking with various articles of differing textures, sizes and shapes and the residents had to guess what they were. Not terribly popular — I don't think they liked the title!

Bingo cropped up from time to time. Just because a game was popular at some specific time in the Home it did not follow that it would be popular forever more. Patterns changed almost daily and enthusiasms waxed and waned depending upon the clinical climate of the bodies and minds. For several weeks one of my cooks and her friend played Bingo with the residents on a weekly basis until the enthusiasm for it wore off. From time to time over the years it was resurrected for short bursts.

Most people — the uninitiated — would view Bingo as a totally sedentary game. Not for us. For us it was a time of maximum exercise. Overseeing two, three or four residents at a time — each carer dashing from resident to resident, keeping the discs in the correct positions and repeating the numbers over and over again. Then someone sneezed or took a deep intake of breath or sighed — and there were the discs, scattered all over the room. Shaking fingers and shaking laps didn't help either.

Nor did the teasing of a certain gentleman. '32' would sing out the caller. 'No' he'd say, 'not got that.' '19', said the caller. 'No, not got that.' '47.' 'No.'

'There is no need to say ANYTHING if you haven't got the correct number', snarled the lady whom it was his intent to annoy. '88.' 'Yes, got that. Two fat ladies – I've got that. 'Don't say that. DON'T SAY ANYTHING.'

Time for the 'heavies' to move in and sort out the problem, while balancing a couple of boards about their persons as they move. All is peaceful for a while. Two and a half cards later . . . '2.' 'Not got that.' '90.' 'Top of the house — no I've not got that.' '41.' 'No.' 'SHUT UP.' '53.' 'Yes.' 'Oh really!' Throws card on floor and storms out of room.

By that time the room had divided into two. Half supporting the gentleman and the other half, the lady. More entertaining really than the Bingo! Much more! Collect up the boards and give out the prizes before there is a general exodus. Everyone needing the toilet at exactly the same time. Again.

And so to the two parties which the Home held each year. The spring luncheon party and the Christmas afternoon tea party.

The Christmas tea, held about a fortnight before Christmas, originated so that the residents (most of them ladies at that time) could once again be hostesses to their families just like they used to be. Sit at the head of an individual table and be 'mother'.

It was a very happy but hot occasion. Being midwinter we could not overflow into the garden so we had to contain ourselves in the lounge or dining room. The rooms were very, very full, so with the invitation went out the warning to wear summer dresses (or the equivalent, if a man!). For my part I had to remember to switch off the heating earlier in the day. The staff had decorated the Home a day or so previously and it sparkled and glittered — gold, red and green. Curtains drawn back revealing the lights, decorations and tree, inviting those outside into the warmth and love that was emitting from the Home. This was the start of all those special visitors — carol singers, little children performing Nativity plays, members of the far-flung family whom perhaps they had not seen since the last bank holiday.

What should we wear for the party, for Christmas Day? Which pieces of jewellery? The men were interested in the first two questions but not the third. Most residents loved it but not all — for some this was the season of sadness, longings and regrets. These had to be recognised and supported. Mostly by loving arms around frail bodies.

The spring party originated as an annual 'thank you'. Thank you to the residents for being there, when they could once again become 'mother' or 'father' of their own table. Thank you to their relatives and friends for all their support. Life would have been so much more difficult without them. I often wondered if they really realised how important they were to the Home and how much support they gave us. Thank you to the staff (who often invited their own guests for this occasion) and thank you to the locals who had also supported us over the year.

It was a moveable feast with the date being decided only when we could trust the weather. No question of every one eating inside on that occasion with upwards of 80 people expected. It was frantic once the decision had been made. So much cooking to do, so much drink to get in. Staff brought in extra umbrellas, tables and chairs. Many came in early to help set it all up. If one ever wondered if all the work that the garden engendered was worth it, the answer was a whole-hearted 'yes'. It was alive and buzzing with voices, chattering, laughing, teasing and munching. It lasted for only about two or so hours, being held mid-week. Many visitors had to get away, staff to collect children from school etc. Some visitors to go back to work. Others stayed on in the garden until 4.00 or 5.00 pm. The cooks stayed on after their morning shift serving, waiting, helping with the clearing-up and the carers who were on duty worked themselves into the ground.

Once it was over, everything went quiet. All the residents were exhausted with their heads full of conversation, faces, memories and all they wanted to do was sleep.

Fair enough. Didn't we all!

ROOMS & PASSAGES
finding the way

'Welcome to the college', boomed out the voice of the lecturer.

It was the first day of the City and Guilds Level 3 Advanced Management for Care course, an excellent course and one which I attended for a year prior to being registered to manage my own Home. It was divided into three sections — Client Care, Management Care and Environmental Care.

Client Care helped us to understand more fully the problems of old age — physical, mental and emotional. It dealt with the needs and wants of elderly people, their aspirations and expectations as well as the importance and compilation of care plans, and many, many more subjects all related to the residents, their relations and background.

Environmental Care made us aware of the rules, regulations and facts relating to food hygiene, the importance of sensible, special diets, safety in the Home and fire requirements. When a Home is initially set up it has to adhere strictly to all the regulations of the Environmental Health and Fire Authority requirements and it has to alter and change throughout the year to comply with new and up-to-date demands. The Registration Authority oversaw the Home as a 'whole'.

Management Care was the section I knew least about before commencing (and possibly when I finished as well) because it dealt with the legal side of running the Home. It also dealt with marketing, finances, advertising, insurance matters and claims, the financial setting-up and everyday running of the Home and the many facets of staffing the Home.

It was an excellent course and the knowledge which I gained from it was what my Home was based upon. It ran through my everyday work within the Home like a ribbon, tying up all the practical experience I had gained from working as a grass-root carer plus attending the numerous courses related to caring for elderly people.

But now back to the first day of that course. None of us at that time knew each other, the layout of the college, which floor we should be on and what format the lectures would take.

I suppose we were rather like residents going into a Home for the very first time.

Except, of course, we could see, hear, talk, observe and then . . . get in our cars and drive away again! 'Are you confused?' 'Yes.' 'Do you know your way around?' 'No.' 'Well, don't worry. You will always be on this floor and luckily it is the only floor which is carpeted.' 'Phew!' 'You will do well to remember how you felt today, any of you who are still designing your Homes, or are involved in setting-up a Home.'

It was the first and probably one of the most important lessons I learnt.

It is so easy to overlook the important role passages and corridors play in a Home or any large building.

After all, they just connect one room or space to another. Don't they? Yes but they need to be user friendly. One needs to know how and where one is going. Never more so than in a Home. Well lit, bright and friendly. Plenty of grab-rails and plenty of distinguishing features. Pictures of different size and subject matter, mirrors, windows and open areas. It is no good having a passageway which no one dare walk along on their own in case they get lost. The name and number on the door is not enough, the picture on the side of the door, or on it, has to be distinctive enough to remember, or the cluster of ornamental fruits or even the fire extinguishers — they all act as an aid to the memory. A lot of residents have to be escorted wherever they go anyway but what about the fleet of foot? They were free to go back and forth to their room when they wanted or to the toilet or kitchen or visit another resident.

A dark, ill-lit, bland area is often too off-putting and residents tended to stay put — missing out on more exercise and more stimulation.

One lady had a wall-hanging next to her door. She knew exactly where to go and how much energy she needed to get there. She thought it was a Persian rug and loved its colour and texture. In fact it cost very little and came from a well-known department store — but who cared? It served the same purpose.

In another passage there was a picture I particularly liked. Not for its artistic merit but for its subject matter. It was just a garden gate surrounded and, in part, hidden by overgrown ivy and greenery. Many years before I had lived in a house with a walled garden which had THAT door. It meant nothing to anyone else but I loved it. It was in one of the general areas of a passageway. If I had been a resident I would have wanted it by my door. I would have certainly known where I was!

And I am quite sure that a lot of the many, many pictures in the Home had the same sort of importance to the residents. Even better if they came from their own home. Less likely to walk on by.

On the whole residents mingled in the lounge in the daytime but come the evening, they were quite happy to retire to their own rooms. Rooms filled with their own pictures (sometimes lovely watercolours painted by daughters or nieces), photographs, ornaments, small pieces of furniture — all intimate to them.

Knitting, tapestry, writing poetry, sharing a whisky with a friend, cassettes and tapes played, reading novels, reading The Bible, prayers, radio, television, receiving visitors, writing letters — all this and more went on in their rooms.

Wilf in particular loved his cassettes. He would sit in his room in the evenings singing and humming to them. Once he started on a cassette, he played it over and over again, until fed-up with it. I remember it so well! His room was close to my office and just along the corridor from Elisabeth's room. One cassette was a compilation of several well-known classics including the national anthem of the country from which Elisabeth had come. He loved this particular cassette and played it loud and clear. Loud enough for her to hear it and, like a beckoning finger, it called her to his room. But old age is so unkind at times — by the time she had located her stick, got herself into an upright position and got halfway to his door, that particular track had finished and it had raced ahead to Ravel's *Bolero*, leaving her looking totally bewildered. I made a mental note to get her out of her room in plenty of time but before I could do so he had tired of that particular tape and gone on to Jim Reeve. This did nothing for Elisabeth nor for me because Wilf had an urge to beat Jim to the end of the song. Each evening I would sit in my office tying up the loose ends of the day, willing Jim to beat him. Just once. 'Go on, go on, Jim, you can do it.' But he never did. And Elisabeth never got toWilf's room in time for her national anthem. Freedom of movement? Sometimes old age just got in the way!

Sport on television blended together many of the residents. Horseracing and snooker were the main favourites along with football — ladies as well as gentlemen. If, however, there was a major match taking place in the evening then the gentlemen liked to watch in their own rooms, away from all the distractions females threw at them. Bathed and in their pyjamas and dressing gowns, drink in hand, well before the start so that the game did not have to be disrupted for such mundane things, they settled down for an exciting evening.

Being engrossed in the current game that one is watching is not absolutely essential. Just being in the atmosphere revives old memories and legs which can no longer stampede over the pitches and courts can still, in the imagination, cover as much ground as the present day professionals.

'Oh good, it will soon be Wimbledon.' Dee would chant frequently during the weeks of May into June. She became a hermit for that fortnight, seldom leaving her room. Even had her meals in front of the television. Totally happy and no trouble. In between she nodded and catnapped her day away. She didn't care who was playing or that rain had stopped play and she was watching games from previous years. In reality she wasn't watching other people play — Dee was playing herself. All those wonderful years of tennis at the club, on lawns and private courts. The boyfriends. The strawberries and cream. And more boyfriends. Afterwards the cucumber sandwiches . . . for she came from that age and background. Henman and Rusedski meant nothing to her — just to see the scenes, hear the familiar sounds were all she needed. If only Wimbledon could have lasted for 52 weeks! No aches or pains that fortnight. Not even a hiccup!

One of our ladies seldom vacated her room. Her eyesight, hearing and movement were restrictive and she could not cope for long with groups of people. She needed quietness. Quietness in which to think, pen poetry, write letters, revive memories and meditate, being deeply religious. Her brain and mentality were generally spot-on. She was terribly adverse to anything or anyone unfamiliar coming in or going on in her room.

From time to time the electrician or plumber were required to rectify faults or breakdowns in her room. Fortunately she liked these two gentlemen and accepted them into her room, being the husbands of members of staff whom she knew well — so she trusted their husbands! They were lovely with her. She liked to know what was going on. She understood what they were talking about, the technical side of it and why they were doing it (which was more than I did). Just because one is in one's 90s does not necessarily mean that one does not understand the intricacies of electricity and plumbing!

At night these thoughts would have gone round and round in her head, building up, querying — so much better than worrying about her physical disabilities.

Yes, it was good to mingle in the lounge, but when evening and night time came, tucked up in one's own room with all one's special mementoes was a special time. Warm, comfortable and doing exactly what one wanted to do — and it was nothing to do with anyone else!

CHOOSING A HOME
it's all relative

Which Home and where? Sounds easy enough — plenty of choice.

Yes there is but there are important factors to be considered before placing one's parent in one. Some find the best way to tackle parents very old age, dependency, confusion and forgetfulness is by openly discussing the subject with them, long before they become very old, dependent, confused and forgetful. Long before they say, 'are you trying to get rid of me?' or, 'are you trying to tell me something?'. Long before, while still rational, clear thinking and unselfish.

That, of course is all right if there is a strong loving bond between parent and carer. Not all families enjoy this state of affairs. Some relationships have to be handled with kid gloves. Some therefore cannot bring themselves to broach the subject and that goes for both parent and children. Some conversations are too emotive.

When is the best time to start looking at Homes? Answer: before you actually need one. While there is time and not so much pressure. So often the carer is faced with having to tear around Homes at break-neck speed, needing a place for their parent — yesterday! No time to go out and do the nitty-gritty rounds of choosing.

When selecting a Home take time to assess the general feelings, ambience, interests, happiness — the smell of the Home in fact. On so many occasions I have heard residents' relations say, 'when looking for a Home, we know the minute we walk through any front door whether or not this is the Home for our loved one.'

Many Homes look beautiful and inviting. Make as sure as possible that what goes on in them is equally beautiful and inviting. This applies to all types of building. Try to remember that a Home which is fine for someone with all their faculties is not always appropriate for someone whose faculties are sadly diminished.

Observe carers and attitudes towards their residents. Observe the appearance of residents — clean, spotless clothing, well-shaven faces, state of finger nails. Are there, in fact, enough staff to care thoroughly?

If you really like the Home, ask if your dependant's name can go on a waiting list — the place to be accepted when you are ready for it. Of course one has to check very well again when the time comes. Owners, managers, attitudes may have changed in the ensuing months . . . going on years.

This would be all right if life was perfect — having all that time, I mean, in which to wander around at one's leisure. If only! So much already with which to fill one's time without worrying about something that might never happen! So many current things to be squeezed into the already overflowing life. So much already with which to fill one's time without worrying about something that might never happen, especially if one realises that nation-wide the percentage of elderly people needing full time or respite care is comparatively small. The majority of people can quite adequately remain in their own homes or warden controlled flats, supported in various degrees by professional carers, health care providers, relatives, neighbours and able-bodied spouses.

In the meantime, keep your ears and eyes open. Listen and question. Seriously — look at several Homes. After all, the one of your choice might not have a vacancy when one is needed. Look at different types of Homes.

Someone used to living in the middle of a town with all the noise and excitement is not going to settle as easily in the middle of the country as someone who already enjoys the rural setting. Some like 'homey' Homes, others more stately. What about the outlook? Outlooks are so important — they allow the spirit (if not the body) to escape from those four walls.

Talk to your parent's social worker (if they do not already have one call the local Social Services department so that an appointment can be made for a social worker to call to assess your parent). What support, funding will there be on offer? They can talk you through the whole procedure, give information, facts and in so many cases, moral support during a very difficult time.

Examine as many options as possible. Sometimes it is very obvious to the family carer that the time has come for their parent to go into full-time care. They or their community carers have done a magnificent job keeping them in their own homes or in sheltered accommodation for as long as possible until it is no longer appropriate. Sometimes it is not quite as obvious until the cries for help are emitted.

Cries for help come in many guises. The constant removal of aids that are meant to ease any disability, incontinency, constant ringing the family, especially in the night, deliberate falling or bruising themselves and so on. The cries initially going out to the carers to be answered.

Be guided by the medical/social services as to whether 'care' or 'nursing' is required but remember you probably know your mother/father's needs and likes better than anyone else. Also remember: do ask your parent (if lucid) what THEY want to do. You may be pleasantly surprised at their answer.

Unfortunately other branches of the tree of that particular carer might also be calling for help at the same time. In-laws are often of a similar age, therefore if one elderly parent is experiencing difficulties, parents-in-law of the carer are often in the same or similar state. As people live longer the children of the octogenarians and nonagenarians are often themselves in their late 50s, 60s or even early 70s.

Caring for their parents at a time in their lives when they would like to be taking it easy or after many years of full-time work, wishing to travel, indulge in hobbies. Then there are the grandchildren (great-grandchildren of the potential resident and far enough removed not to be of any great concern to them). But grandchildren of the carers are a different matter. Helping their children with school runs, babysitting, shopping and so on. Being pulled in every direction at the same time.

Essential, therefore, that the resident goes into full-time care or at least respite, before the carer goes 'ping'. There seem to be very fine lines between the feelings of relief, guilt and sadness — often the three emotions fusing into one.

On many an occasion I have had a carer (usually the daughter) in my office or on the end of the telephone silently weeping with relief when I tell her I have a vacancy for her parent. At the end of their tether, no more strength, no longer able to think straight, their marriages feeling the strain and on the receiving end of resentment from the extended family. Utter exhaustion. Looking after an elderly relative does not only involve shopping, cooking etc, but physically moving them and supporting and transferring them. When both the physical and the inner strength which supported all that for as long as was necessary is no longer needed, then the tears flow. No more strength left to hold them in. Utter relief.

Then utter guilt. Why do the children feel so guilty? Not admittedly all, but most! They have loved and supported their parents for as long they were able. They feel they are letting them down by not continuing to do so.

Is it because those children in their 60s and 70s can still remember their own childhood when the grandparents lived with or in the house next-door to them and they felt they should do the same? If their parents did it for their parents should they not also do it? Maybe the next generation will not have such a hang-up. Loving, supporting as long a possible — and wise and right for the parents — but accepting help at the relevant stage and not having those past images impregnated into their memories.

Is it, perhaps, deep down that some of the elderly parents expect their children to look after them as they did their parents? In my grandparents' day, the spinster gave up work to go home to look after the parent in need — as did widowed daughters. It was generally accepted. Nor will the next wave of very elderly people think of residential Homes as the 'workhouse' — the stigmas of which still live on in the minds of some. In their youth, the extended family often only extended to the extremities of the village or to the next town. On call to assist. Nowadays the extended family has extended itself to the shores of this island, onwards and outwards and now covers the world.

No matter how loving/caring/how many telephone calls or visits are made by brothers and sisters from away, it is not as debilitating nor does it encroach on their everyday life to the same extent as the one doing the 'hands-on' caring. Twenty-four hours a day.

So many different facets to this problem. Children living many miles away from their parents with no one to hand apart from the social services team who assess the needs and put in the required level of care. The father of one of my friends, an only daughter, lived 200 miles away from her. His only son lived in Denmark. She arranged for the social worker to call. 'No', he said when she arrived, 'I don't need any help, my daughter looks after me.' Two hundred miles away!

When first taken ill she visited him Friday night until Sunday night. Every week. 'No,' he said in ignorance, 'I don't need help.' His daughter certainly did though! Social services returned and set-up relevant schemes — assistance with dressing and getting-up and retiring to bed. He also received meals on wheels and control of medication. He moved from private residence to a warden-controlled flat, the daughter now visiting every month or whenever he had a hospital or clinic appointment. He was happy but then started falling and bumping into things. His daughter never 'switched off'. 'No', he still said, he was all right and did not need to go into residential care.

At home she spent her time telephoning, arranging, analysing her father's health. In between she helped her husband run his business, her daughter gave birth to another baby, which in turn generated more babysitting. She too had a small part-time business to run. Fitting in extra visits as often as possible to her father. And still she felt guilty!

Ought she have him at home with her? How would he get upstairs? How would he manage in the bathroom? How could she go out and leave him? He had no friends and no background there. Eventually she persuaded herself it was to her father's benefit for him to go into care in his home town, amongst his 'roots'. She had loved and cared for her parents for many, many years — just as they had done for her all her life. And maybe that is why she still felt guilty and extremely sad. Sad because this person who had always been such a tower of strength to her was now infirm, hard of hearing and no longer able to enjoy life to the full and she longed for him to be young again and to be the Dad he used to be.

Most of our residents lived within a ten mile radius of the Home. Not too far for visitors to call and not too far a drive for the resident to be taken back to lunch. Extended families, friends of the family, living nearby. Staff who already knew the resident or their families. Familiar country-side, familiar voices and dialects. Most importantly, many residents able to retain their own doctors, social workers and other members of the various medical teams who came into the Home.

It was predominantly a village Home for village people. I don't think a city dweller would have been happy there, although some residents came from afar. In retirement they had moved to live with or near to their children, building up their own circle of friends and acquaintances and were happy with their adopted 'roots' and were also happy to move into the local Home.

Some came to us from . . . anywhere. They came to us for a limited period of time — their families needing them close so that they could pop in whenever needed and through-out the day. The resident not too worried about being part of the community outside — they would not be going out anyway. They were just happy to be near their loved ones when they knew they would not be with them for much longer and to be looked after and at ease.

Only two people did not stay through choice. It was right for them not to. One came from the north of England and one from Scotland. The Scottish lady, in particular, was still mobile enough to go shopping and walking on her own. Her family lived nearby and they had moved her down so that she could share their lives — have her over at the weekend. But when she went out she knew no one and she longed for the freedom of her home town where she could walk around the streets greeting well-known faces. She longed to hear again the well-loved Scottish accents. Be able to talk about things past. With us she could not join in with the general conversation about local issues. Not only that but we couldn't produce any mountains for her!

She had the choice — stay and see her family very frequently or move back and see them once every six to eight weeks at the most. For the next period of her life she chose to go back and she and her family and we were pleased that she had been able to make that decision. In a way it was as if she had had 'respite' with us and it was used to it's full value. The other lady also missed her native tongue and countryside and knowledge of all things local but happily for her, her family were eventually able to move back and take her with them and place her in a Home there.

There could be no hard and fast rules — each potential resident and their family had their own specific requirements. Very often it was knowing what the best answer was in theory, for the parents but in practise this was not acceptable, too impracticable and too difficult to balance the equation for the carer. If the situation could be accepted with love and understanding on both sides and a genuine wish for the agreed decision to succeed, then it could work.

It was so easy for an elderly person, cocooned in a Home, to forget the pressures that they themselves were under when so much younger. Bringing up a family, working to support them and all the stresses of everyday life. In the Home, so much of that stress now eased away. So easy to forget and not understand and criticise. Again, this is a generalisation — many do remember.

Visitors played a big part in the lives of residents in the Home, none more so than their own visitors — sons, daughters, sons and daughters-in-law, grandchildren and great-grandchildren, old friends, vicars and so on. These were the strands of life that formed bridges from their old home to their new Home. They were not completely cut-off. They were not abandoned.

So often visitors to one resident found they knew others in the Home. The visiting circle and the circle of conversations and reminiscences widened. It was good as so often it encompassed those who did not have quite the back-up that others enjoyed.

There was nothing nicer than walking into the garden on a warm, sunny day and finding a lot of visitors sitting with their own but also mingling too with other residents. It always turned into a mini garden party — lots of conversation, laughter and no one feeling left-out. It wasn't previously arranged — it just happened. As indeed it did on dreary spring, summer, autumn and winter days when everyone was confined to the lounge. Some of the happiest moments just happened.

No indeed, not all visits went according to plan. A mother or father could quite easily nod-off five minutes after the visitors arrived, having travelled for an hour or so to see them. Some relations — certainly not all — thought that the need to visit and telephone was not so important with their relation safe and sound in a home. Not so — the outward and visible signs of loving and caring were still of paramount importance and without them the resident could feel abandoned and unloved. No matter how high the level of caring nor how good the home, these things could in no way compensate in the resident's mind for what they really wanted. Elderly parents can still criticise children's lifestyles and ask, 'why don't you visit more often?' can still remonstrate and upset them and point out the danger and folly of their ways, even if that child happens to be in his or her 50s, 60s or even 70s. Is it to make them feel guilty or just a bad day? Could be anything but visiting days did not always overflow with happiness.

And then the resident died. No more visitors relating to that particular lady or gentleman. Over the weeks, months and years the visitors became an integral part of our lives and were our friends. Everyone promised to pop in, but few did. It was so understandable although we would love to have seen them. Maybe it would have evoked too many memories, afraid to interrupt the routines of a busy day, afraid someone would be on duty they didn't know and not understand why they were there. Busy lives enveloping them once again.

For whatever reason we lost a thick layer of visitors, both personal and also from the support teams. Doctors, district nurses, social workers, dentists and so on. Anyone from that list attending that certain resident stepped back and did not necessarily attend the next resident to come in. But eventually coming in again in whatever order to attend to another's problems.

But the relatives — that left a gap in our lives for a while. The daughter who sat every Saturday afternoon, knitting, keeping her mother company unless she took her out. The daughter and son-in-law who visited every Sunday afternoon. Nieces who visited on Thursdays and daughters who came in the afternoon on most days some having walked in from the village, spouses who walked to us from across the fields — almost on a daily basis becoming an integral part of the home. Grandchildren, sons, daughters who visited regularly and frequently but at no specific time. No more telephone calls for a certain person. Gaps on Sunday evening at 6.00 pm from Scotland. Gaps at 8.30 am on a Saturday from a brother in Norfolk. Gaps from just about everywhere in the country. And then someone else filled that gap and we too remustered our working lives.

STAFF

the supporting cast

'In the meantime', I said to my newly appointed member of staff, 'you will wear a leotard'.

'Right', she said, looking dubious.

It was interview time a few weeks before the opening of my new Home.

In training, during the management section of the Advanced Management for Care course which I was attending at the local college, my peers and I were required to role play the art of interviewing. I'm sure we learnt a lot, were alerted to the pitfalls and legalities of the job, but role playing in the classroom cannot be compared with the real thing. For obvious reasons it could not but it introduced us to the subject so that we were not quite so 'green'.

The interviews took place over three days — for carers, cleaners and cooks. I was so nervous and reluctant to start, that prior to taking the interviewees to my office I employed delaying tactics and escorted them around the house discussing different aspects as we went. Discussing, questioning, observing and getting as much feed-back as I could before going into the dreaded office and conducting a 'proper' interview.

So nervous was I that Mrs Malaprop was reincarnated during those three days and she never really left all the time I ran my Home. We were discussing uniforms, my new carer and I. I thought we should choose the style between us at a later date and in the meantime had bought several tabards for the job. 'Leotards' slipped out by mistake during the fifth interview — my nerves not having been quelled. On two other occasions the next day I said the same thing when, sadly, I was concentrating very hard on NOT saying 'leotards'.

'Am I really sure I want to work there?' the three asked themselves after the interview. 'And if I do, who provides the rabbit ears and puffball tail?' or so they told me several weeks later when the newness of our acquaintance had worn off and it doesn't leave much to the imagination as to what their remarks were when, several years later, I asked if they would work in that 'bordello'.

In some respect the naked fear experienced in those early days paid off. Forevermore I started my interviews by walking the potential member of staff around the Home, introducing them to fellow workers, watching and observing reactions to situations, interactions with residents, their knowledge of various hoists, lifts, appliances, problems that we came across on the way round. One learnt a lot from seemingly casual and relaxed conversation and usually by the time we reached the office, I knew whether or not I wanted that person to work for me and whether or not she would fit in with the rest of the established team. So by the time the interviewee settled down to be interviewed the interview was over. All I needed were references that needed to be checked, knowledge of courses, exams and experiences and personal information.

As the years went on 'The Interview' became more of a formality. Present staff recommended friends, neighbours, relations and anyone they knew of the right calibre and personality. Of course I still had to interview them but they had not come in from the cold with neither side knowing the other.

Another plus emerged as the years rolled by. Previous employees returned to the fold, having left for all sorts of reasons — ill-health, returning to the area, having moved away for a while, time off to nurse sick parents, sisters, children and so on. This was wonderful — they knew the system and Home intimately and even still knew most of the residents and staff. If there weren't the hours available when they applied to return they took what was on offer, covered for sickness and holidays and in no time at all had built their hours up again. In the main there was a stable regime of staff. This was good as continuity, dependability and familiarity (at the correct level) was of paramount importance to the residents. And most certainly to the Home owner/manager!

At the same time it was good that from time to time someone left. Not because I wanted them to, on the contrary, but it did leave openings for fresh faces, fresh ideas and fresh attitudes.

It is so easy for a residential home to become completely insular. Established methods sometimes need to be adapted. New ideas, attitudes needed to update them. A nice slow trickle of staff keeps the Home from becoming stagnant. Respite residents have the same effect. Visitors and visits, likewise. Life should not stand completely still. On the other hand, staff and ideas should not changed too rapidly — a trickle is infinitely more acceptable in every way than a 'river (or even canal) in full flood'.

My carers, cooks and cleaners were all of equal importance. There could be no weak links or lesser links in the chain. If that were so it would break or snap. They were all paid the same, were liked and respected by the residents and their relations and each other to the same level. What use is good caring if the bath seats, toilet seats and commodes were dirty? What good is it having residents with dietary problems if the cooks could not make acceptable meals for them? What was the point of the cooks getting it right if the carers fed the residents whatever they wanted or if they did not clean up after residents had been to the toilets when the cleaners weren't there? No point at all.

In every home the hub is usually the kitchen. So it was with us. Not the cooking area but way back by the patio doors which led out to the sunroom. Here there was a large farmhouse type table and chairs and this is where the business of the day went on. It is essential to have up-to-date care plans for each resident. These are the bases on which we endeavoured to maintain their wellbeing. To bring the plans alive, healthy discussion has to infiltrate them.

This was the time when, gathered around the table, thoughts, concerns, comparisons, anxieties about a resident were expressed. And concern, worries and anxieties from the residents themselves. Their health seldom stayed still, always moving upwards or downwards. How could we improve their lot? Could we involve the relations more, would they benefit from this or that?

Staff are able to go away, switch off the problems of the Home — back to their own lives. But time and time again a good idea would be born in the middle of doing the ironing or while idling at a red traffic light. Out of the blue! One to be explored, discussed. Doctors, nurses, medicines, the backbone of their health requirements did so much for the betterment of our residents but sometimes it was just a thought put into practice which could make so much difference to their emotional and possibly their physical lives — overlapping as they did.

It was around the table that we bounced ideas off each other — the staff, myself, residents' relations and whenever possible the residents themselves. It was also around the table and in the kitchen that the malapropisms flowed fairly freely. Especially later on in the evening when tired and usually when talking to a visitor, which was even more embarrassing. If they weren't too bad my staff could control their laughter, mostly just going red and eyes running but I always knew when I had excelled myself because when I looked around, the room would be completely empty. 'Aromatics' would become 'aerobics', 'insulated' to 'isolated' and so on.

It was also around the table that friendships between members of staff were cemented. Some shifts overlapped each other by half an hour mainly so that extra help was at hand at especially busy times but it was also a time when more in-depth verbal reports could be given complimenting the routine written ones. The table ensured that all shifts knew each other. There could not be any 'them and us' syndrome. No night versus day or morning versus afternoon or evening shifts. It was a place where general chatter, if time allowed, took place.

This was when any personal problems came to the surface and where they could 'let off steam' if the need arose. This was when comfort or appreciation could be expressed. Staff supported each other — lifts were given to and from work, shifts taken over at short notice in emergencies, telephone calls made to the ill. They played, drank and relaxed together. And it was good.

No, of course there wasn't **always** a friendly atmosphere. Thirty females all working closely together meant there were occasionally the odd problem. differences of opinion mostly on work-related subjects — ie. attitudes, efficiency and abilities. Around the table these could be brought to light at an early stage, discussed, evaluated and often nipped in the bud and resolved.

If personal problems developed between members of staff they had to be kept at arms' length from the Home until they too were resolved. All my staff took a professional pride in their work. Carers, cleaners and cooks. There was no room for the 'lick and promise' attitude — not from themselves nor tolerated from the rest of the shift.

As well as their own specific jobs, staff undertook extra duties on behalf of the Home, often involving their husbands too. Once a year a group of staff, under the leadership of one specific lady, hired the local community hall and ran a mammoth Bingo session. It was supported and attended by large numbers of villagers and staff — all proceeds going to the Home for the benefit of the residents. Prizes given by many of the local businesses, shops and staff. They made a lot of money. This was banked for outings, drinks, lunches and extra presents at Christmas, given out by Father Christmas. Entry to all entertainment, concerts and shows — all were free, all could go. It took a lot of hard slog. One room of the organiser's home was buried under an avalanche of prizes.

Other staff, cooks and cleaners as well as carers, helped physically with the outings, concerts and clubs. Several helped with transport. Others took home knitting to correct, alter dresses, shopped for the residents if they wanted something out of the ordinary.

Once a year after the children had gone back to school after the summer holidays a group of staff would get together to commence rehearsals for the Christmas Eve entertainment which was performed before the residents, their relatives and friends and any members of staff, not on duty, who wanted to watch.

A different theme was used each year. Different songs and different costumes. Each week they met in each other's homes, rehearsing and sewing. The result was brilliant. One of our resident's granddaughters accompanied them on her electric organ. The rehearsals were great fun — and another bonding session — all to the good of the Home.

Sherry, whisky, wine — alcoholic and non-alcoholic — mince pies and indigestion tablets were all served in the interval on that Christmas Eve.

Our electrician, heavily disguised as Father Christmas, ho, ho'ed his way amongst the residents distributing the presents. His full-time job was being married to one of our cooks. Our plumber kariokee'd his way through the interval while the 'heavenly choir' performed a quick change of outfit. His full-time job was being the husband of one of our carers and father to my wages clerk.

Father Christmas was assisted in his task by a quick-change carer in shimmering and sparkling fairy outfit, sequinned long johns just peeping seductively out from under short skirt, frilled and sparkling, wand in hand and tiara on head. Skipping around all over the place!

The idea of the concert was born in the first year of our opening. One lady in particular, the fairy, worked very hard to get it going but for one reason or another it didn't get off the ground and was shelved until the next Christmas. I don't think that mattered. What was important was that it brought a group of people together with a common aim who hadn't previously known each other very well outside the Home. It formed a good nucleus on which to build.

Training was an important aspect — not just the in-situ, in-house sessions but the many and varied outside courses that the staff attended, — handling and transferring, fire, first aid, food and hygiene, entertaining the elderly, understanding dementia and so on, whether they were taking their NVQs or not. They also served another purpose — my staff met staff from other Homes, exchanged ideas and discussed problems. More breaths of fresh air for the Home.

Being in the Home most of the time or in our private house which was attached to the Home and with my office in the centre of the Home, I could see and hear most of what went on. But it was so easy to become blasé when employing a very capable staff. So easy to become complacent and even lazy.

For two years I produced diaries of the day to day running and special events that had occurred in the Home during that year for the interest of my staff. During one summer, unknown to the staff, I conducted a survey for a week, an in depth awareness of the functioning of the Home and the wellbeing of the residents. Here is an excerpt from one of those diaries:-

It was an unusual week for that time of the year because every member of staff was present — no holidays and no illnesses. Therefore, what I am going to say applies to you all. It was a fairly representative week when four of you had personal problems of such enormity that they virtually took you over. Three more of you were coping with an on-going situation with other large problems and I suspect that the rest of you had the usual variety of everyday traumas with which to deal — like everybody else.

It was the same week in which one of our carers became engaged to be married and when another of you became a grandmother for the first time.

It was the week of the spring luncheon party, a resident's birthday party and an evening of entertainment by a local group.

It was the week in which one of our regular respite visitors (staying with us at the time) mourned the death of a very dear sister.

It was a week in which comfort, support, both verbal and practical, was given to those who needed it by all of those who knew about it.

It was a week in which great joy was shown to those who deserved it — by those who were in great distress themselves as much as anyone else.

It was the week in which the bereaved lady was able to weep for her sister in privacy and/or the comforting arms of an assistant and, on the evening of the funeral, which also happened to be the evening of the entertainment, she thanked her carer while being put to bed and said she had had a very happy evening.

Personal problems can easily colour one's attitudes towards one's work. I looked very closely and saw no evidence of this. On the contrary, I saw a week in which all the residents were happy, contented, amicable (well, mostly!), physically as well as usual, relaxed and mentally stimulated. This is the yardstick by which I measure the strength of my staff — carers, cleaners and cooks.

In the week when you were all present, there were no second class staff, only those of the first class variety.

Many times in the ensuing years I repeated this in-depth level of observation — when I stood back and tried to look dispassionately as an outsider and assessed my staff. Each time the result was the same, although the events were different — the basic work being done every day was of the same standard. If faults came to the surface they could usually be traced back to management!

It is easy to comprehend the general work of what goes on in a communal Home — washing, transferring, cooking and serving of meals, laundry, dressing, putting to and getting up from bed, general cleaning — all that is easy to understand.

Medication to be given out, rigid adherence to their medical requirements as directed by the doctors and nurses, special diets to be seen to, changes to care plans at any given moment and to be updated. Then there were the residents' own personal likes and dislikes, needs and wants — all of which change like the wind. Add to that general counselling and sorting-out problems, arguments and upsets etc. So many facets to each resident. Not least of all attending to toilet needs and bathing the residents with respect and understanding. One never knows when or where, from one minute to the next, one will be required. No, caring is not for the squeamish. Those who do it WELL are very special people.

I'm not sure when it was that I lost my staff. It came to me suddenly one day that there were none left — only supportive and loving friends. We laughed, discussed, worried, cried and every other emotion put together for what we hoped was the betterment of the Home and happiness of our residents.

Yes, of course it was stressful, wearying and many more negative words like that – but my goodness it was fun a lot of the time. And the tears we cried were not all of sorrow but of happiness and silliness and sheer stupidity. Many, many times we just prolapsed with laughter or do I mean collapsed?!

These were the friends who threw birthday parties for me, cooking all the food, buying all the drinks, inviting residents and their relations and members of the community, as well as involving my family in the secret. The first for no special reason, the second was when I received my official 'bus pass'. It was the staff who organised the superb leaving party when my husband and I retired. This time only residents and staff were invited, the staff again providing the food and drinks. Most of the residents went to bed at their usual time, but one lady stayed up through the night, dancing the hours away with the staff. Just because one is in a wheelchair it doesn't mean one cannot dance the night away. And after operations it was my staff who waited on and bullied me into keeping away from work and 'doing as I was told'.

Telling someone that I was 'insulated' instead of 'isolated' I suppose was not too bad. Telling someone that I was 'nubile' instead of 'mobile', certainly was.

Nubile? ME! NUBILE?!!

I looked behind me.

The room was completely empty.

It was time to go.

May 1998

Courses/Resources
(See Useful Addresses)

Age Concern Training — A wide variety of one & two day courses relevant to people working in homes or day care. Free brochure available

Age Exchange Reminiscence Centre — training in reminiscence, also publications and resources (reminiscence boxes etc) as well as theatrical productions based on memories.

City and Guild — courses leading to qualifications in management and caring.

EXTEND — Movement with music for over 60s and disabled people of all ages. Training available plus a list of local teachers.

JABADAO — courses (specially for those working with older people) on the role of movement in communication & well-being, simple practical ways of working with movement

National Association of Providers of Activities for older people (NAPA) — concerned with establishing appropriate practice regarding the provision of activities for older people. Provides regular themed 'Sharing Days' and quality training (including courses on working with dementia sufferers). Further information on courses is available from the Director of Training: Tessa Perrin, 12 Walter Way, Silver End, Witham CM8 3RJ. 01376 585 339

National Vocational Qualifications (NVQs) — in management, caring etc. Contact you local College for details.

BOOKS   (SEE *USEFUL ADDRESSES*)

See organisation's free catalogues for other relevant publications

Age Concern Books   Publications aimed at those working with older people. Titles include: *CareFully: a handbook for home care assistants; Nutritional Care for Older People; Dementia Care; Health and Safety in Care Homes; Reminiscence and Recall;* and *Good Care Management: a guide to setting up and managing a residential home* etc.

Gardening in Homes: a guide for relatives in nursing and residential care homes.   Published by **Relatives and Residents Association**

A Better Home Life: a code of practice for residential and nursing home care. Published by the **Centre for Policy on Ageing**. The most comprehensive guide available to standards in care homes. Also *Trained to Care? The skills and competencies of care assistants in homes for older people*

Leisure, Later Life and Homes by Alison Clarke and Jackie Hollands. Published by **Counsel and Care** - information and ideas on a diverse range of activities for older people in care.

More than Movement for Fit to Frail Older Adults - Creative Activities for the Body , Mind and Spirit by Postiloff Fisher. **Jessica Kingsley,** 116 Pentonville Road, London N1 9JB

Reminiscence: Social and Creative Activities with Older People in Care by Roger Sim, published by **Winslow Press,** Telford Road, Bicester OX6 0TS. Tel: 01869 244644 Winslow also provide materials for activities.

Useful Addresses

The following information was correct at the time of printing.

Age Concern England
1268 London Road
London SW16 4EJ
Information Line
0800 7314931

Age Concern Cymru (Wales)
4th Floor
Cathedral Road
Cardiff CF1 9SD
029 2037 1566

Age Concern Ireland
114-116 Pearse Street
Dublin 2 Ireland
+3531 677 9892

**Age Concern
Northern Ireland**
3 Lower Crescent
Belfast BT7 1NR
01232 245 729

Age Concern Scotland
113 Rose Street
Edinburgh EH2 3DT
0131 220 3345

Age Exchange
Reminiscence Centre
11 Blackheath Village
London SE 3 9LA
020 8318 9105

Alzheimer's Society
10 Greencoat Place
London SW1P 1PH
020 7306 0606

**Association of Independent
Care Advisers**
58 Southwick Street
Southwick, Brighton BN42 4TJ
01483 203 066

Carers National Association
20 Glasshouse Yard
London EC1A 4JS
020 7490 8818
Carers Line 0808 808 7777

Centre for Policy on Ageing
25-31 Ironmonger Row
London EC1V 3QP
020 7253 1787

Christian Council on Ageing
c/o Epworth House
Stuart Street
Derby
DE1 2EQ

City and Guild Head Office
1 Giltspur Street
London EC1 9DD
020 7294 2800

**Counsel and Care
for the Elderly**
Twyman House
16 Bonny Street
London NW1 9PG
020 7485 1550/1566

CRUSE Bereavement Care
Cruse House
126 Sheen Road
Richmond
Surrey TW9 1UR
020 8940 4818/332 7227

The Disabled Living Centre
(for details of local Centres)
Redbank House, 4 St Chad's
Street, Manchester M8 8QA
0161 834 1044

EXTEND 22 Maltings Drive,
Wheathampstead
AL4 8QJ.
01582 832760

Help the Aged
St James's Walk
Clerkenwell Green
London EC1R 0BE
020 7253 0253
SeniorLine 0808 800 6565

Jabadao, Branch House
18 Branch Road, Armley,
Leeds LS12 3AQ
0113 2310650

**National Association of
Providers of Activities for
older people (NAPA)**
5 Tavistock Place
London WC1H 9SN
020 7383 5757

**The Relatives and Residents
Association**
5 Tavistock Place
London WC1H 9SN
020 7916 6055

**The Royal National Institute
for the Blind (RNIB)**
224 Grreat Portland Street
Londonn W1N 6AA
020 7388 1266

**The Royal National Institute
for Deaf People (RNID)**
19 - 23 Featherstone Street
London EC1Y 8SL
020 7296 8000

Requirements for Home owners and managers

In 1984 the Registered Homes Act came into being. Since then local authorities have issued their own specific guidelines based on this Act. Health care expertise, although required, is not sufficient proof of ability, on its own, to run a business. Being *au fait* with employment law and having a good general understanding of the needs of elderly people is also expected.

Each Home has an annual inspection day with as many unheralded visits as the Inspection Officer feels is necessary to monitor the Home and to offer guidance when needed. Action against the Home can be taken if necessary. Residents and potential residents and their relations have open access to these reports.

The Registered Homes Act is under revision and the existing guidelines are being examined by the government as this book goes to print. The National Required Standards are very detailed and will, when agreed, be consistent for all local authorities.

Anyone considering opening or managing a residential Home should, before buying or altering a building or indeed spending time and money on lengthy training, contact their local Inspection Service Office to ascertain that the building would be fit for the purpose and that the location, access and amenities are acceptable.

It is required that a Home owner (when the manager is a different person from the owner) visits the Home at least once a month and is diligent in overseeing good care and conduct within the Home.

For advice on National Vocation Qualifications (NVQs) in care at all levels, contact your local college.

PH 4/2000

What do you say when people tell you that activities are not important?*

Tessa Perrin, NAPA Course Director

What can we do to make certain that activities do not get sidelined? Those of us who are in the position of delivering therapeutic activities need to be able to give good account of ourselves. Our work is generally perceived as a luxury, not as a necessity (ie. life threatening if we don't do it) and we need to be able to offer a convincing argument to those who see it this way, if ever we are to be able to make progress. I actually believe that to neglect therapeutic activity **is** life-threatening and this article is intended to offer some pointers as to the kinds of arguments we need to arm ourselves with. Essentially, it is a matter of responding to two sets of questions.

1. What happens to people when (for whatever reason) they stop engaging in activities?
Physical changes:
- muscles atrophy and joints develop contractures
- bone loses calcium leading to osteoporosis and fracture
- heart atrophies and blood pressure increases
- risk of thrombosis and embolism increases
- appetite diminishes
- gastro-intestinal movement decreases and constipation increases
- potential for urinary infection increases
- potential for respiratory infection increases
- potential for decubitus ulceration increases
- sleep pattern is disrupted

[It may be of interest to know that joint contractures start forming after only 8 hours of inactivity; muscle atrophy, bone loss and heart changes after only a few days of inactivity]

Psychological changes:
- decreased alertness
- diminished concentration
- increased irritability, impatience and hostility
- increased tension and anxiety
- listlessness and restlessness
- depression and lethargy
- feelings of oppression
- problem-solving difficulties
- confusion and disorientation

[It may also be of interest to know that these changes start to take place within 48 hours of inactivity]

The experience of inactivity has been described in various terms, which are perhaps best summed up as 'extremely debilitating'. An eminent gerontologist has coined the term 'a mental bedsore'. Others have used the term 'bored to death', a phrase we often use in a flippant manner, but actually containing a deep truth. Prolonged inactivity can, and often does, lead to physical and psychological ill health, vegetation and death.

2. What happens to people when they do engage in activities? We can best examine this by looking at the changes that take place following a period of inactivity .

Physical changes:
- muscle strength and joint mobility increases

- bone loss diminishes and healing time of fractures reduces
- blood pressure and potential for thrombosis and embolism diminish
- appetite increases
- gastro-intestinal movement increases and defecation normalises
- continence improves
- potential for respiratory disorders decreases
- potential for skin disorders decreases
- sleep pattern normalises

Psychological changes:
- smiling, laughing and talking increases
- initiation of, and engagement in, social interaction increases
- alertness to environmental stimuli increases
- concentration and memory improve.
- emotions are more readily expressed
- agitation diminishes and relaxation increases
- humour is manifest
- self-assertion increases
- self-expression is enriched
- ability to give and receive affection increases
- daily living function is improved

It is necessary to add a note that although all the above changes have been noted in research, many people, in residential settings particularly, come to activity after severe occupational and sensory deprivation, often over a very prolonged period of time. Many of the people we meet are physically and psychologically very damaged. The extent therefore to which they will be able to make changes in the above areas will depend upon the extent and nature of the damage. Not everyone will show changes in all these areas. Nevertheless, almost everybody has the potential to make some changes in some areas.

A sentence of death?

What then do we say to the person who says that activity is not a priority for care settings today? Well, it may sound melodramatic, but we have a good foundation for stating quite unequivocally, that sentencing a person to a life of inactivity, is tantamount to a sentence of death. The health care world has difficulty understanding this. Health care understands that if we do not feed a person, or keep them warm and sheltered, or pick them up when they fall, or dress their wounds, they will sicken and die. It understands this because the sickening and dying take place very quickly following failure to meet these basic needs. It fails to understand that sickening and dying are also a consequence of inactivity, simply because the former are often so far removed (chronologically) from the latter. Death by inactivity is a slow, prolonged, agonising annihilation, often over a period of years. The sooner the healthcare world makes the connection between activity and health, and inactivity and sickness and death, the sooner will we be enabled to offer our clients true quality of care. But all this depends upon you and me, upon knowing what we are about, and being able to declare what we are about. This is how attitudes will change.

*Re-printed by kind permission of NAPA

THIRD AGE PRESS
. . . a unique publishing company
inspired by older people

. . . an independent
publishing company which recognizes that the
period of life after full-time employment and family
responsibility can be a time of fulfilment and
continuing development
. . . a time of regeneration

Third Age Press

. . . books are available by direct mail order from
Third Age Press or on order from good bookshops.
All prices include UK p & p. Please add 20% for other
countries.   UK Sterling cheques payable to
Third Age Press.

6 Parkside Gardens London SW19 5EY
Phone 020 8947 0401   Fax 020 8944 9316
e-mail: dnort@thirdagepress.co.uk
Website: www.thirdagepress.co.uk
Dianne Norton ~ Managing Editor

Registered in England Company Number 2678599
VAT registered 627 9627 01

On the Tip of Your Tongue:
your memory in later life

by Dr H B Gibson . . . (a mere octogenarian himself) explores memory's history and examines what an 'ordinary' person can expect of their memory. He reveals the truth behind myths about memory and demonstrates how you can manage your large stock of memories and your life. Wittily illustrated by Rufus Segar.

Includes:

What is memory? The four memory systems. Different sorts of memory.

How is your memory changing? Meeting people. Mistaking physical for mental change. Remembering to do things.

The 'Tip-of-the-tongue' phenomenon - Breaking the blockage. The puzzle of blocked recall. The Freudian explanation.

Gimmicks for remembering: Mnemonics - Place method - Pegwords - learning foreign words - 'chunking' - list of memory aids.

Improving your memory - Memory training. A practical training course. What kind of memory have you got?

Will you continue to make progress all your life? Memory at different stages of life. Enemies of progress. Reminiscence.

Derangements, diseases and injuries that effect memory. Brain damage, amnesia, depression, senility, Alzheimer-type conditions.

1995 160pages   ISBN 1 898576 05X £7.00

Buy this book together with *A little of what you fancy* for only £13.00

A Little of What You Fancy Does You Good: your health in later life

by Dr H B Gibson ~ illustrated by Rufus Segar

'Managing an older body is like running a very old car - as the years go by you get to know its tricks and how to get the best out of it, so that you may keep it running sweetly for years and years' . . . so says Dr H B Gibson in his sensible and practical book which respects your intelligence and, above all, appreciates the need to enjoy later life. It explains the whys, hows and wherefores of exercise, diet and sex ~ discusses 'You and your doctor' and deals with some of the pitfalls and disabilities of later life. But the overall message is positive and Rufus Segar's illustrations once again bring whimsy and insight to a very readable text. Dr H B Gibson gives due cause for optimism.

Includes:

How much exercise do you take? - Determinants of fitness. How fitness can be regained in later life.

What about diet? - The constituents of food. Miraculous food & food additives. Can diet increase your life span?

What about sex? Myths about sex in later life. What sexuality means in later life. Shyness.

You and your doctor - Different types of patients. The doctors' dilemmas with older patients.

Some pitfalls in later life - Eating - drinking - smoking. Personality types.

Disability in later life - phyical conditions, sensory loss, dementias, depression, bereavement, loneliness etc.

1997   256 pages ISBN 1 898576 £8.50

An Experiment in Living: sharing a house in later life

by June Green, Jenny Betts & Greta Wilson

A new lifestyle for a new millennium's thirdagers? Truthful, humorous, thought-provoking, considered and practical . . . . this book is an introduction to a potential new lifestyle by three wise women. With 39% of women between the ages of 65 and 74, and 58% of those over 75 living alone, June, Jenny and Greta asked themselves some searching questions about how they wanted to face the future and came up with a sensible and exciting answer.

Starting with - *Do you really want to share a house?* - they take the reader through all the practicalities (sometime worked out the hard way!) involved in finding the right house and turning it into a home where they could all pursue their own interests while, at the same time, providing each other with support and friendship.

But the book is more than just a guide to how to set up house together. Interspersed with the practicalities the three authors have each reflected on *What's in it for them* and their individual attitudes to retirement. Candid friends and young relatives give their views of the arrangements and other options for shared living are also considered.

Maggie Guillon's cartoons cleverly pick up the delights and dilemmas of shared living.

1999 132 pages Pb ISBN 1 898576 14 9 £9.25

Consider the Alternatives: healthy strategies for later life

by Dr Caroline Lindsay Nash   Illustrated by Maggie Guillon

This book offers a clear and unbiased explanation of the nature and uses of a wide range of alternative therapies . . . what you can expect of complementary medicine . . . and why yoga, pets, music and humour can contribute to your personal strategy for a healthy thirdage. There are also contributions from Dr Michael Lloyd, a psychologist specialising in the management of pain, and from pensioner, Tony Carter, on how and why he thinks you should take control of your own health.

Maggie Guillon's cartoons add a delightful touch.

Includes:

• *Alternative techniques of diagnosis*

• *Physical therapies - external body* - Back pain, chiropractic, cranio-sacral, physiotherapy, acupuncture, zero-balancing, Alexander technique

• *Physical therapies - internal body* - Nutrition, macrobiotics, herbalism, colonic irrigation

• *Mind over matter* - Psychoanalysis, psychodynamic counselling, humanistic approaches, psychosynthesis, counselling, group therapy, family therapy, transactional analysis, hypnotherapy

• *Something for the spirit* - Past life therapy, meditation, spiritual counselling, spiritual healing, reiki, psychics and mediums

• *A holistic view of health* - Homoeopathy, anthroposophical medicine, traditional Chinese medicine, Ayurveda

• *Exercise and relaxation* - Exercise, dance, yoga, tai chi, massage, tragerwork, shiatsu, aromatherapy, pets

• *The strange, rare and fun* - Flower remedies, crystal healing, colour therapy, feng shui, drama, art and music therapy, laughter

1998 160pages ISBN 1 898576 11 4 £7.00

Changes and Challenges in Later Life: learning from experience

Edited by Yvonne Craig
Foreword by Claire Rayner ~
illustrated by Maggie Guillon

Older people share with those of all ages the desire for fulfilment - a need to transform surviving into thriving. This book brings together experts from Britain's major caring organisations to share their wealth of experience and practical advice on the sometimes difficult situations of later life. The wealth of experience concentrated in this book shows how changes and challenges can lead to positive attitudes and action.

Contents and authors

• *Legal rights and remedies* **Barbara Beaton**, Age Concern Legal Unit

• *Neighbours* **Yvonne Joan Craig**, Elder Mediation Project of Mediation UK & **Archana Srivastava**, Stirling University

• *A good ending* **Gillian Dalley**, Centre for Policy on Ageing

• *Mistreatment and neglect* **Frank Glendenning**, Centre for Social Gerontology, Keele University

• *Making the most of change* **Mervyn Kohler**, Help the Aged

• *Who cares?* **Jill Pitkeathley**, Carers National Association

• *The right retirement home* **Rudi Reeves**, Advisory, Information & Mediation Service for Retirement Housing

• *Care homes, residents and relatives* **Jenny Stiles**, The Relatives Association

Maggie Guillon's drawings give a humourous perspective to each chapter.

1997 160pages ISBN 1 898576 10 6 £7.00

Lifelines . . . *is a series that focuses on the presentation of your unique life. These booklets seek to stimulate and guide your thoughts and words in what is acknowledged to be not only a process of value to future generations but also a personally beneficial exercise.*

by Eric Midwinter

A Voyage of Rediscovery: a guide to writing your life story

A Voyage of Rediscovery is a 'sea chart' to guide your reminiscence. It offers 'triggers' to set your memory to full steam ahead (although backwards might be more appropriate) & provides practical advice about the business of writing or recording your story.   **1993 28pages ISBN 1 898576 00 9 £4.50**

Encore: a guide to planning a celebration of your life

An unusual and useful booklet that encourages you to think about the ways you would like to be remembered, hopefully in the distant future.   **1993 20 pp ISBN 1 898576 02 5 £2.50**

The Rhubarb People . . . Eric Midwinter's own witty and poignant story of growing up in Manchester in the 1930s.

. . . is published as a booklet but also as a 90-minute audio cassette read by the author. The cassette includes useful tips on writing or recording your story.

  1993 32pages ISBN 1 898576 01 7 £4.50 ~ audio cassette £5.00

Getting To Know Me . . . is aimed at carers and families

of people in care. It provides the opportunity to create a profile of an older person ~ their background and relationships, likes and dislikes, as well as record the practical information needed to make the caring process a positive experience for all con-cerned. The end result should be a valuable tool for any carer.

            1996 24pages   ISBN 1 898576 07 6 £4.50

Lifescapes: the landscapes of a lifetime
by Enid Irving

. . . introduces a whole new art form . . . a 'Lifescape' is a collage of memories. Make one just for fun or as a very special family heirloom. Lifescapes can be made by individuals, in groups, as a family or as an intergenerational activity. This latter approach is particularly recommended for people in care working with students or young helpers. The resulting Lifescape is not only decorative but serves to increase understanding of the whole person and stimulate memory.

1996 24pages   ISBN 1 898576 08 4 £4.50

For Carers ~ *Voyage* has been particularly popular with individuals wanting to get started on their own life stories but the comprehensive guidelines can equally well be used by people working together. For those working with more frail people *Getting to know me* is especially designed to create a profile of an individual in care or about to go in to care.

To create a more visual record of a life and, at the same time, stimulate memory and communication, Enid Irving has developed the unique concept of the *Lifescape*. The guidelines can be used by an individual, by two generations working together by a carer or artist working with a frail older person, or by a group. *Getting to know me* & *Lifescape* work very well together to create a comprehensive picture of an individual. *The Rhubarb People* makes an excellent reading-aloud book and stimulates reminiscence ~ or hear the author read his own story on the **90-minute audio cassette**.

No Thanks to Lloyd George:
The forgotten story ~ how the old age
pension was won

by Dave Goodman   Foreword by Jack Jones

. . . a new edition of this popular book to celebrate the 90th
anniversary of the Old Age Pension Act. *No Thanks to Lloyd
George* tells a story of passion, dedication, determination and
grit. From 1898 old people, living in fear of the work house,
thronged to packed meetings all over the country to hear how
their lives could be transformed by the introduction of a pension. But it took more than ten years of struggle and disap-
pointment before the first British old people collected five
shillings from their post offices.

1998   96pp   ISBN 1 898576 12 2   £3.60
Bulk orders of 10 or more copies are £3.00 each

Europe at Walking Pace

by Ben & Betty Whitwell   . . . inspiring **and** practical . . .

can be used as a guide for long or short walks or put your feet up and enjoy the wonderful descriptions of the off the beaten track places that these adventurous walkers reached and the detailed observation of the countryside that you only get at walking pace.

Ben and Betty Whitwell retired early, rented out their home, loaded up their backpacks and set off to walk through France, Spain and Portugal — following some of the Grand Radonné routes and the Santiago de Compestela Pilgrim's Way and sometimes just getting lost!

Their imagery is strong enough to rouse the most dormant wanderlust. The ordinary and extraordinary people they encountered, the pitfalls and the pleasures, are related with frankness and humour.

1998 264 page ISBN 1 898576 13 0   £9.25